Physical Characteristics
Belgian Shepherd D

(from The Kennel Club breed standard)

Body: Body powerful but elegant. In males, length from point of shoulders to point of buttocks approximately equal to height at withers. In females slightly longer permissible. Chest deep and well let down. Ribs moderately well sprung. Upper line of body straight, broad and powerfully muscled. Belly moderately developed neither drooping nor unduly cut up continuing lower line of chest in a graceful curve. Rump very slightly sloping, broad but not excessively so. Skin springy but quite taut over whole body. All external mucous membranes highly pigmented.

Tail: Firmly set, strong at base, of medium length. When at rest, hangs down, with tip slightly bent backwards at level of hock; when moving it should lift accentuating curve towards tip, never curled, nor bent to one side. Tip may be carried slightly higher than topline.

Hindquarters: Well muscled and powerful. Good but not excessive angulation; hocks well let down. Viewed from behind, legs parallel. Dewclaws to be removed.

Feet: Toes arched, very close together; soles thick and springy with large dark claws. Forefeet round. Hindfeet slightly oval.

Size: Ideal height: dogs: 61–66 cms (24–26 ins); bitches: 56–61 cms (22–24 ins). Weight, in proportion to size.

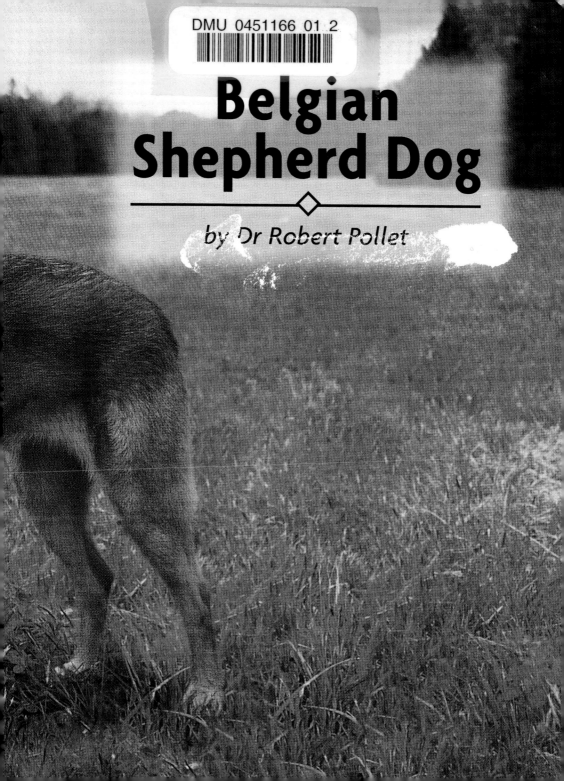

Belgian Shepherd Dog

by Dr Robert Pollet

Table of Contents

9

History of the Belgian Shepherd Dog

Meet the four varieties of the Belgian Shepherd Dog: Malinois, Groenendael, Tervueren and Laekenois, and discover the origins and foundation dogs of each variety. See the breed's popularity blossom in its homeland as well as Britain, North America, the Continent and around the world.

43

Breed Standard for the Belgian Shepherd Dog

Learn the requirements of a well-bred Belgian Shepherd by studying the description of the breed set forth in The Kennel Club standard. Both show dogs and pets must possess key characteristics as outlined in the breed standard.

27

Characteristics of the Belgian Shepherd Dog

Understand the talents of the Belgian Shepherd that make the breed so versatile and successful as a working and guard dog. Are you the right owner for this intelligent, trainable and agile shepherd dog? An active, vital dog that requires stimulation and affection from his owner, the Belgian Shepherd exudes personality and bravery.

52

Your Puppy Belgian Shepherd Dog

Be advised about choosing a reputable breeder and selecting a healthy, typical puppy. Understand the responsibilities of ownership, including home preparation, acclimatisation, the vet and prevention of common puppy problems.

PUBLISHED IN THE
UNITED KINGDOM BY:

INTERPET
PUBLISHING

Vincent Lane, Dorking
Surrey RH4 3YX
England

ISBN 1-903098-56-4

80
Everyday Care
of Your
Belgian Shepherd Dog

Enter into a sensible discussion of dietary and feeding considerations, exercise, grooming, travelling and identification of your dog. This chapter discusses Belgian Shepherd care for all stages of development.

PHOTOS BY ISABELLE FRANCAIS,
WITH ADDITIONAL PHOTOS BY:

Norvia Behling
TJ Calhoun
Carolina Biological Supply
David Dalton
Doskocil
James Hayden-Yoav
James R Hayden, RBP
Bill Jonas
Alice van Kempen

Dwight R Kuhn
Dr Dennis Kunkel
Mikki Pet Products
Phototake
R Pollet
Jean Claude Revy
Dr Andrew Spielman
Riitta Tjörneryd
C James Webb

Illustrations by Renée Low

98
Housebreaking
and Training Your
Belgian Shepherd Dog

by Charlotte Schwartz
Be informed about the importance of training your Belgian Shepherd from the basics of housebreaking and understanding the development of a young dog to executing obedience commands (sit, stay, down, etc.).

127

Health Care of Your
Belgian Shepherd Dog

Discover how to select a proper veterinary surgeon and care for your dog at all stages of life. Topics include vaccination scheduling, skin problems, dealing with external and internal parasites and the medical and behavioural conditions common to the breed.

Index: 156

The Publisher would like to thank the following owners of dogs featured in this book:
Laurie Baker, Steve Beman, John Browne, Denis Court, N Deschuymere, Serge Gillet, Robert Graham, Everett Lewis, Kenneth Mazzie, Claudine Nodin, Sylvie & Stéphane Ramoni, Anthony Rosa, Steve Skolnick, Robert Van Weremael, Sue & Mike Young

A Belgian Groenendael, the black long-haired Belgian Shepherd Dog, is steadily becoming a favourite working dog around the world. The overbreeding that has harmed the German Shepherd Dog has not affected the Belgian breed, making it a preferred choice in many countries.

History of the
BELGIAN SHEPHERD DOG

THE EARLY HISTORY IN BELGIUM

The exact origins of many breeds of dog have never been documented, having existed centuries before the interest in 'purebred dogs' began. While it is not possible to trace the exact origin of the Belgian Shepherd Dog, there is some information available. As the name indicates, the Belgian Shepherd Dog originated as a herding dog. Before the end of the 19th century, more precisely before 1891, the Belgian Shepherd was only known as a working dog for shepherds and farmers, not necessarily as a 'purebred dog.'

Unlike the German Shepherd Dog, whose origin is clearly and inseparably associated with one man, Rittmeister Max von Stephanitz, Belgian Shepherd Dogs were promoted by three dog men, who are considered the founders of the breed, namely the veterinary surgeon Prof. Dr Reul, L Van der Snickt and L Huyghebaert.

On 29 September, 1891, the Club du Chien de Berger Belge (Belgian Shepherd Dog Club) was formed in Brussels. The same year, on 15 November, Prof. Reul

Samlo, a short-haired Belgian Shepherd, brown brindle, is one of the founders of the variety. He is the father of Tomy and the grandfather of Tjop.

Tjop (Tomy X Cora I), a famous Malinois ancestor.

organised a first gathering of Belgian Shepherds from various Belgian counties at the veterinary facility in Cureghem. This meeting was called in order to determine whether a national shepherd dog type actually existed. At this gathering, 117 dogs were presented and it was concluded that there was a consistent type of Belgian Shepherd Dog. From that number, 40 dogs were selected for breeding, all of which were anatomically the same, though their coats varied greatly in length, texture and colour.

The following year, the first Belgian Shepherd Dog speciality

Tomy (Samlo X Diane), the ancestor of the Malinois and the first short-haired Belgian Shepherd with a charcoal fawn coat and a black mask.

show, where all colours and coat types were represented, was organised. It took place on 8 May, 1892 in Cureghem.

The first standard describing the ideal characteristics of the Belgian Shepherd Dog was written in 1892. It described three coat varieties: long-haired, rough-haired and short-haired. This standard has been changed a number of times, leading to

today's standard that describes four varieties. The point of controversy, then as now, has always involved coat length, texture and, especially, colour. These many disputes have hindered the development of the breed.

Another club, founded in 1898 by L Huyghebaert and Dr G Geudens, was located in Malines. This club, in fact, was a branch of the Club of Brussels. At that time, violent disputes and conflicts arose between these two clubs, involving prominent experts of the breed. All of this conflict centred around coat types and colour as well as the emphasis on beauty (conformation) versus the dogs' so-called working value.

Prof. Reul and his Club du Chien de Berger Belge lost this struggle and eventually disappeared. The Berger Belge Club, founded in 1898, remained and was recognised in 1898 by the Royal Society Saint-Hubert. A few

Tom (Vos I X Lieske), rough-haired and with a fawn coat.

years later, the Royal Groenendael Club was also recognised. These two clubs continued their activities until the 1990s. On 30 March, 1990, after many years of effort, they were united. Currently the only organisation responsible for the breed in Belgium is the Royal Union of the Belgian Shepherd Clubs.

Over the years, the number of varieties has changed several times, resulting in the four recognised around the world today: the Malinois, Tervueren,

Groenendael and Laekenois, each of which varies in coat colour, texture and/or length. Nevertheless, the breed characteristics were written down by 1910, which was quite an accomplishment, as the breed type had only been established 20 years previously.

In 1901, the first Belgian Shepherds were registered in the stud book of the Royal Society Saint-Hubert. The first officially registered Belgian Shepherd, number LOSH 5847, was Malinois Vos des Polders, the father of Dewet. It took a good ten years for the Society to begin registering the native Belgian breeds, which

Dewet (Mouche X Vos desé Polders), formed the basis of the Malinois breeding along with Tjop.

Boer Sus (Basoef X Mira), a famous rough-coated ancestor.

Duc de Groenendael (drawing by E van Gelder), the most famous son of Picard d'Uccle and Petite (the foundation couple of the Groenendael variety) and the father of Milsart, which played a major role in fixing the Tervueren type.

were not a priority. The Society was preoccupied at the time with hunting dogs and the more established breeds from elsewhere, like the more 'aristo-cratic' Collie, which had already been registered many years before. The Belgian Shepherd, with the exception of the Groenendael, had been too long considered a

herding dog of the lower classes, who placed greater emphasis on the working capacities of their dogs rather than their physical beauty.

As for the promoters of the breed, one of the best breed experts of the Belgian Shepherds has been Felix E Verbanck. He began to breed Malinois in 1931 (under the kennel name de l'Ecaillon) and researched the history of the varieties. As Secretary of the Royal Groenen-dael Club, he possessed an enormously rich library of information about the breed. As a valued adviser on the breeding of Belgian Shepherds in Europe and

Jojo du Maugré (Iago du Maugré X Ialta du Maugré). Photo by R Pollet.

A nice, typical Malinois at a Belgian dog show. Photo by R Pollet.

the US, he guided very important decisions for the breed. He also wrote numerous influential articles on breeding that are still quoted today.

ORIGINS OF THE FOUR VARIETIES

As the recognised varieties have changed constantly, there inevitably has been much inter-breeding between the varieties. Nevertheless, it is possible to outline briefly the origin of each separate variety.

Gitan de la Terre Aimée (Maubray du Maugré X Alma de la Terre Aimée). Photo by Riitta Tjörneryd.

MALINOIS

This variety has been bred primarily around the town of Malines, whence his name is derived. Trainers and working competitors have always prized the dogs' abilities and their

excellent working character. The Club of Malines specialised in the short-haired variety, and the selection of these dogs was focused mostly on their aptitude as a working dog. This explains why in the beginning many

Sicco de Kersouwe (Maubray du Maugré X Patara van Balderlo). Photo by Riitta Tjörneryd.

Bundessieger Koran van Balderlo (Elton van Banderlo X Iris van Banderlo). Photo by Riitta Tjörneryd.

POST OFFICE SALUTES BELGIUM'S TOP FOUR

On 26 May, 1986, four postage stamps were issued in Belgium to honour the best known Belgian breeds, namely the Belgian Shepherd Dog (pictured, left to right: Malinois, Tervueren and Groenendael) and (not pictured) the Bouvier des Flandres.

Lady de la Casa du Barry (Ch Ino de la Casa du Barry X Ch Fanny de la Casa du Barry). Photo by Riitta Tjörneryd.

with a charcoal fawn coat and a black mask. Tomy was the son of Samlo (short-haired brown-brindle) and the charcoal grey-brindle short-haired Diane. Tomy was bred to Cora van Optewel or Cora I (short-haired brindle with mask) and produced Tjop (short-haired fawn without mask) in 1899. Tomy and Tjop had a good fawn colour. Tjop was considered to be a prototype of the variety and his name can be found in the most important bloodlines of the short-haired dogs.

faintly coloured dogs were bred, but after a while colour directives were followed more closely.

Because the Malinois was the superior competition dog, many cross-variety breedings took place. The Tervueren, especially, owes a great deal to the Malinois bloodline.

The most famous ancestor of the Malinois is Tomy, the first short-haired Belgian Shepherd

A typical, high quality Malinois bitch.

Another famous Malinois ancestor was Dewet. He was related to Tjop, as his mother, Mouche (short-haired silver grey), was a sister of Diane, the grandmother of Tjop. The father of

Dewet was Vos des Polders, the first officially registered Belgian Shepherd in 1901. Dewet was powerful and very coarse. His fawn colouring was very light and his black overlay was disposed in black patches. Tjop and Dewet were two studs of different type, but they formed the basis of the Malinois breeding.

From the end of the 19th century until the present, the Malinois has been the beloved Belgian favourite, which results from the Belgian passion for obedience and protection training. Historically the Malinois has been the working variety, always surpassing the other varieties in trainability and working capacity, which has remained so to the present day.

LAEKENOIS
The origin of the Laekenois, the rough-coated Belgian Shepherd, is closely related to that of the Malinois. They were originally

ADOPT A 'SCHIP' CHUM
For Belgian Shepherd owners seeking a companion for their trustworthy dog, look no further than the Schipperke. It is very noteworthy that when a choice has to be made, the Schipperke is the breed of preference! In France the Belgian Shepherd and the Schipperke clubs even jointly publish the same monthly canine magazine.

A typical, American-bred Malinois.

bred and predominantly found near Antwerp and Boom. The rough-coated male Vos I is considered the ancestor of the short-coated as well as the rough-coated variety. He was mated to Lieske (short-haired brindle), which

15

An American-bred Laekenois.

The Laekenois derives its name from the royal park of Laeken in Belgium.

A closeup of the head of the Laekenois.

produced Diane, the mother of Tomy. However, from the same combination, rough-coated offspring were produced as well,

the most famous being Tom (rough-haired fawn).

Diane was bred by the shepherd Janssens, whose sheep grazed in the royal park of Laeken. His best dogs were fawn and rough-haired. The royal domicile gave its name to this variety, hence the name Laekenois.

The rough-coated ash-grey bitch Mira was sired by Tom (rough-haired fawn), producing Basoef (rough-haired ash-grey), father of the famous rough-coated ancestor Boer Sus (ash-grey).

All these dogs, and also Tony, a very well-known son of Boer Sus, had the ash-grey coat colour. It is, however, the fawn rough-haired dogs of the breeding of the shepherd Janssens that became popular and eventually superseded the ash-grey. This fawn colour became the official

DIAGRAM OF MALINOIS AND LAEKENOIS ORIGINS

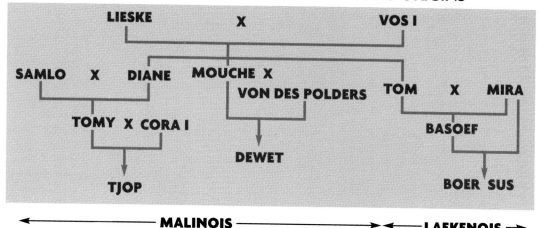

```
        LIESKE              X                    VOS I

SAMLO    X    DIANE    MOUCHE X              TOM    X    MIRA
                       VON DES POLDERS

    TOMY X CORA I                                 BASOEF

                            DEWET

        TJOP                                   BOER SUS
```

◄─────────── MALINOIS ───────────► ◄── LAEKENOIS ─►

colour of the Laekenois and remains so today.

GROENENDAEL

The two long-coated varieties, the Groenendael and the Tervueren, share the same early history so their origins are intimately interconnected. Only since 1899 have they been judged separately at dog shows, as 'blacks' and 'other colours.'

At the first Belgian Shepherd speciality show in 1892, the first prize was given to Petite, a three-year-old black long-haired bitch, who has to be considered the female ancestor of the black long-haired variety.

Picard d'Uccle, a beautiful black long-coated male, who met very well the requirements of the standard decreed by Prof. Reul, was predestined to become the ancestor of the Groenendael.

Bottom, left: Donald Poretta, Laekenois male. Bottom, right: Multi-champion and World Champion Max van Kriekebos (Hassan van Kriekebos X Jody van Kriekebos).

17

most frequently used stud.

Several matings then occurred between Picard and his daughters, between Duc de Groenendael and his sisters, and also between half-brothers and half-sisters descended from Picard. Many dogs from these matings were born in the Chateau Groenendael, the hotel-restaurant in Groenendael near Brussels, owned by the breeder Mr Rose, whose kennel was de Groenendael. This stock formed the basis of the 'long-haired blacks,' officially given the name Groenendael in 1910.

A lovely Groenendael puppy.

The hauntingly beautiful head of the Groenendael.

Picard and Petite were purchased by Nicolas Rose. Picard was regularly bred to Petite, becoming the foundation pair of the Groenendael variety. On 1 September, 1892, their first litter was born, including Baronne, Mirza, Pitt, Bergére and Margot, as well as the well-known Duc de Groenendael, who became the

An American-bred Belgian Groenendael.

TERVUEREN

The Tervueren, the long-haired 'other than black' Belgian Shepherd, was for a long time treated as a poor cousin of the Groenendael. It has been asserted incorrectly that this variety is a crossbreeding of the Groenendael and the Collie. According to L

Huyghebaert, Groenendaels and Tervuerens have such a mutual relationship and a common origin that they cannot be separated. They are indeed the same dogs, only differing in colour.

The Tervueren owes his name to the village of Tervueren, the home of the breeder M F Corbeel, who, around 1895, owned two fawn-coloured long-haired dogs, Tom and Poes, commonly considered the foundation breeding pair

An American-bred Belgian Tervueren.

champion. He had a deep charcoal fawn coat and has been described as a perfectly successful prototype of the variety. He is the real forefather of the charcoal fawn long-haired Belgian Shepherd. His pedigree demonstrates the common origin of the two long-haired varieties, regardless of colour, since all long-haired progeny definitely go back to the black foundation couple Picard d'Uccle and Petite. Indeed, Tervueren born from

The Tervueren is a long-haired Belgian Shepherd that is 'other than black.'

of the variety. They produced Miss, a fawn bitch with good black overlay, who was unquestionably regarded as the ancestor of the Tervueren variety.

Milsart, the result of the union of Miss and the black Duc de Groenendael, son of Picard and Petite, played a major role in fixing the Tervueren type. In 1907 he became the first Tervueren

As a puppy, the Belgian Tervueren possesses a softer coat than the adult.

19

DIAGRAM OF GROENENDAEL AND TERVUEREN ORIGINS

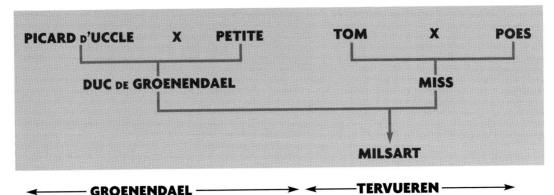

PICARD D'UCCLE   X   PETITE   TOM   X   POES

DUC DE GROENENDAEL   MISS

MILSART

← GROENENDAEL → ← TERVUEREN →

Groenendael parents have played an essential part in the development of the Belgian Shepherd in Europe.

From this short survey of the early history of the breed it should be clear how logical it is that the Belgian Shepherd Dog is classified as one single breed. The four varieties, the result of intermatings, are indeed only different appearances of one and the same dog.

THE BELGIAN COUSIN: THE SCHIPPERKE

It is is generally accepted that the Belgian breed known as the Schipperke, a wholly black little shepherd dog (Schipperke means 'little shepherd' in Flemish dialect), and the Belgian Shepherd have a common ancestor in the Leuvenaar. This extinct Belgian breed, whose name means 'inhabi-

The Belgian cousin, the Schipperke, is known as 'the little shepherd' and has been employed for various tasks, from herding to ratting.

tant of Louvain,' was an all-black lupoid dog, which weighed between 10 to 12 kgs. From this common stem, the smallest have been selected as rat-catchers (Schipperkes) and the largest for herding and guarding livestock (Belgian Shepherds).

THE BELGIAN SHEPHERD DOG IN BRITAIN AND IRELAND

In 1931, the first Belgian Shepherd Dogs, the Groenendaels, were brought to and recorded in Britain. After World War II, Groenendaels were imported from Belgium and France in 1959, 1964 and 1966. A most significant import from Belgium was the bitch Peggy de la Baraque de Planches. In 1971 Quentin, a son of Peggy, became the first British champion.

In 1965 the Belgian Shepherd Dog Association was formed in the UK. At that time, only the Groenendael variety was in the country because it had been decided to import only the black long-haired Groenendael, not the red long-haired Tervueren, to avoid confusion with the long-haired German Shepherd Dog. In 1972 the first Groenendael arrived from America and from 1975 on, new and regular imports came from Belgium and France.

The Tervueren arrived later in the UK. In 1971 the first imports came from France and also from America. In fact, the early development of the Tervueren in Britain was dominated by American imports, which differed in type from the Continental dogs. The American dogs lacked overall elegance and had less refined heads. Fortunately, more imports from Belgium during the years from 1978 to 1983 had a great

At the famed Crufts Dog Show, this handsome Belgian Shepherd Dog was awarded Best of Breed in 1999.

Hassan van Kriekebos (Max v.d. Schepershoeve X Floride de l'Apache). Photo by R Pollet.

Multi-champion Opium van Kriekebos (Ch Max van Kriekebos X Karanelle van Kriekebos). Photo by Riitta Tjörneryd.

impact and the quality of British Belgian Shepherds was markedly improved.

The Malinois, the short-coated variety, was first imported in 1972. This variety became much appreciated in Great Britain but was never as popular as the long-haired Tervueren and Groenendael.

The rough-coated Laekenois were first imported from Holland

in 1980 and have remained, as in every country, the least popular variety.

Today, the Belgian Shepherd Dog in Great Britain has attained a position and a status that is enviable in the canine world. The founder members of the Belgian Shepherd Dog Association who encouraged the growth of the

A very typical head of a Laekenois (Hassan van Kriekebos).

breed never expected the tremendous success the breed enjoys today.

In Ireland, the first Belgian Shepherd Dog, a Groenendael, was registered in 1969 and the Belgian Shepherd Dog Club was formed in 1976. The first Tervueren was imported from the UK in 1980 and the first Malinois in 1986, also from the UK. Recently, more imports have come not only from the UK but also from France, Norway and

Holland. In Ireland, also, the future of the Belgian Shepherd looks bright.

THE BELGIAN SHEPHERD DOG IN THE US AND CANADA

In almost all countries around the world, the four varieties are recognised as being one breed. However, in 1959 in the United States it was decided to recognise three separate breeds: the Belgian Sheepdog (Groenendael), the Belgian Tervuren (Tervueren) and the Belgian Malinois. The Laekenois, unfortunately, is denied recognition and registration by the American Kennel Club (AKC). Note that the Americans

Tequilla van de Duvetorre (Ch Opium van Kriekebos X Qwini van Kriekebos.) Photo by Riitta Tjörneryd.

refer to the breed as 'Sheepdog' instead of 'Shepherd' and that the AKC spells 'Tervuren' without the second 'e.'

The fame of the Groenendaels spread after World War I, during which they distinguished themselves by their working abilities on the battlefields, serving as message carriers, ambulance dogs, etc. The first Groenendael arrived in the States accompanying returning American soldiers, who had seen and admired the Belgian Shepherds when serving overseas during World War I.

The Belgian Sheepdog Club of America was formed in 1919. Unfortunately, between the two World Wars, the Great Depression

Valkohampaan Athene (Hassan van Kriekebos X Fiona Poretta). Photo by Riitta Tjörneryd..

23

of the 1930s dramatically decreased the popularity of the Groenendael and the Club ceased to function. After World War II, during which the Belgian breeds had again impressed by their talents as a war, defence and guard dog, the interest in the Groenendael was rekindled and the breed had a new start, thanks to many Belgian, and also a few French and Italian, imports. The current Belgian Sheepdog Club of America was formed in 1949.

The first Belgian Tervuren was registered in 1918, but by the time of the Depression the variety had disappeared from the AKC stud books. In 1953 the fawn long-coated dogs were again imported. The American Belgian Tervuren Club was established in 1959.

Few people realise that, after the devastation of the breed during World War II, America—almost as much as France—helped to recreate the Tervuren. Unfortunately, the European experts called the revived breed the 'American type of Tervueren,' which is heavier, longer and more angulated.

The first short-haired Belgian Shepherds were registered in 1911. Although after World War II the Belgian Malinois did not flourish, there was still a renewed interest in the dog. The real surge in popularity came from 1963, and since 1965 the Malinois has been eligible to compete for

championships. New imports and increased breeding activity since 1973 made its presence better felt, but the Malinois, the most popular of the four in its homeland, is numerically still small in the States, where it is the least popular of the three recognised Belgians.

In Canada, in accordance with the practice in the European countries, only one breed is recognised, the 'Belgian Sheepdog,' which includes all four varieties. Although the breed had been owned and bred in Canada for many years, it was not until June 1964 that the Belgian Sheepdog Club of Canada was formed.

THE BELGIAN SHEPHERD DOG ON THE CONTINENT
In most countries on the Continent, there has been remarkable progress in the popularity of the Belgian Shepherd Dog during the final decades of the 20th century. The breed is very important in France, Switzerland, Italy, the Netherlands and the Scandinavian countries.

In Belgium, the Malinois is still the most popular variety, followed by the Tervueren, the Groenendael and the Laekenois. However, in many other countries of Europe, such as the Scandinavian countries, the Groenendael has always been the most popular. However, in the period between

1980–1990, the situation changed when the number of registrations of the Tervueren surpassed that of the Groenendael.

In France, the Belgian Shepherd Dog is numerically stronger than in Belgium. All over the world the quality of the French breeding is considered to be the equivalent of that in Belgium. The French primarily love the long-haired varieties of any colour. The Belgians first registered the long-haired fawns, but the French in a certain sense created the Tervueren variety.

In the Netherlands, Belgium's northern neighbour, the Belgian Shepherd has always been very popular, despite the existence of their own official national breed, the Dutch Shepherd Dog. Indeed, in Holland there have always been amateurs, primarily those interested in police and defence trials, who are enthusiastic about the Laekenois, the variety which has been abandoned by the other countries, including Belgium unfortunately. We can even assert that we owe to the Dutch breeders a debt of gratitude that the Laekenois still exists.

As for Germany, the dominant position of the German Shepherd Dog is evident. However, it is not generally known that the Malinois ranks very high as a working dog in Germany's military service. The breed most frequently used as a police and a service dog (customs,

DUTCH COUSINS

The Belgian Shepherds have many admirers in the Netherlands despite that country's indigenous herding dog, the Dutch Shepherd. This handsome herder occurs in three coat types, long, rough and short, just like its neighbour, the Belgian. The breed is more colourful, including blue, grey, yellow, silver and various eye-catching shades of brindle. Of the three varieties, the short coat is the most popular, though all three are unfortunately very rare, even in Holland.

Shorthaired

Roughhaired

Longhaired

border patrol, tracking, etc.) is, of course, the German Shepherd, but the Malinois occupies the second place, before the Rottweiler and other working breeds.

THE BELGIAN SHEPHERD DOG AROUND THE WORLD

The Belgian Shepherd Dog is known and appreciated not only in Europe and America but also on other continents. In Japan, there exists a lively interest in the breed and there have been frequent imports. In Australia, a lot of breeding has been carried out and many imports came from Europe. Speciality shows are regularly organised by the breed clubs, which already have been judged several times by breed-specialists from Europe. In South Africa, Belgian Shepherd Dogs were first registered in 1966. The South African Belgian Shepherd Dog clubs are very active and maintain good contacts with the mother country of the breed.

On the set of *Through the Back Door*, here's a famous Hollywood trio, Charlie Chaplin, Mary Pickford and Douglas Fairbanks, posing with a Belgian Shepherd used in the film. The silent film was shot in 1921.

Characteristics of the
BELGIAN SHEPHERD DOG

Dogs are the most intimate companions of man, having served him faithfully for thousands of years. Over 300 different breeds are recognised today and all of these breeds share a fundamental virtue, their loyalty to man. Nevertheless, each breed has its own personality and characteristics.

Boris de la Pouroffe (Yako de la Pouroffe X Vallia des Forges Monceux), a Groenendael male dog. Photo by R Pollet.

dogs, called the Pastoral Group in the UK. The herding dogs always have been and still are the faithful companions of the shepherd, helping him to lead the flock to the pastures. They bring back the

Ch Buddy van Lana's Hof (Mistyk van de Hoge Laer X Blackie de la Grande Lande). Photo by Hans-Jürgen Fischer.

The psychology of a breed can be understood best in terms of the work for which it was intended to do. The Belgian Shepherd Dog belongs to the group of herding

Louky de la Quièvre (Ch Kadour de la Quièvre X Holenka de la Quièvre), a Groenendael male dog. Photo by Riitta Tjörneryd.

Ch Uzo de la Poumiroffe (Jason de la Douce Plaine X Ch Quiryna de la Poumiroffe), a Groenendael male dog.

sheep that have strayed and defend the flock against attacks by wolves and other wild animals.

The Belgian Shepherd can be described as strong, agile, quick, intelligent, watchful and trainable. These qualities explain the breed's impressive versatility and usefulness for all kinds of canine sports, training disciplines and service-dog education.

Ch Falk von Nauenhof, a famed Belgian Groenendael male dog.

PHYSICAL TRAITS

To be able to do their job properly, shepherd dogs should be of medium build. Their physical appearance and traits are sometimes called 'lupoid,' which means 'wolf-like.' The erect ears, pointed muzzles and bushy tails are typical of these dogs. The largest shepherd dogs are nowadays used as guard dogs as well as defence and police dogs. Shepherd dogs, provided they are physically and temperamentally sound, are considered to be among the easiest of all dogs to train, given their keen loyalty to man, intelligence and desire to please.

In the past Belgian Shepherds were bred for herding ability, but an increasing interest in dog shows made the breeders pay closer attention to appearance. Everybody has to admit that the general appearance of the modern Belgian Shepherds is very appealing. The diversity in coat and colour has given rise to a division in the so-called varieties. With four beautiful Belgian Shepherd varieties from which to select, everyone can find a dog which appeals to him/her.

The best known variety, at least in Europe and especially in

Belgium, is the Malinois, the short-haired variety, whose unexaggerated, simple appearance is still very elegant. The Malinois is greatly renowned for its exceptional ability as an all-purpose working dog.

The Laekenois is the rough-haired variety, with hair made to resist the inclement weather conditions. His outstanding character and trainability have always been greatly admired. It is a pity, however, that his popularity is inversely proportional to his positive qualities. The variety has excelled as much as any of the others in police work.

Next to these two strong but elegant working chaps, we have the real lords, the aristocratic black Groenendael and the magnificent Tervueren, which, with their splendid coats, create a majestic impression. The red or fawn Tervueren with black overlay is considered by many the

Ranke de la Quièvre (Ch Kadour de la Quièvre X Fripouille d'Artamas). Photo by Riitta Tjörneryd.

most beautiful of the four varieties.

However, let us never forget that according to the standard no variation is acceptable in the structure and type of the four varieties. This simply means that, apart from the coat, all four varieties should be entirely identical.

When comparing the physical appearance of the Belgian Shepherd with other shepherd dogs that are its nearest relatives, it is obvious that very important anatomical characteristics, such as its rather light skeleton, moderate angulation and overall elegant appearance are most favourable for a working dog. As a matter of

Ch Buddy van Lana's Hof (Mistyk van de Hoge Laer X Blackie de la Grande Lande)1, a magnificent Groenendael male dog. Photo by Hans-Jürgen Fischer.

Belgian Shepherd Dog

The UK Champion and winner of Crufts Group (1992), Vallivue Bon Chance (Ch Norrevang Bacchus of Belamba X Ch Snowbourn Enchantress of Vallivue).

fact, its speed is impressive and its ability to jump (high and broad) and climb an obstacle, a wall or a ladder is unequalled.

PERSONALITY

The character of the Belgian Shepherd Dog is truly his trump card. His behaviour sets him apart from other shepherd breeds. His rapid reflexes, impulsiveness, emotionality and hypersensitivity are very distinctive.

His 'qualities of character,' which are vital for his success as a working dog, find expression in his general appearance and have been described as follows in the author's *Blueprint of the Belgian Shepherd Dog*: 'The sparkling temperament of the Belgian Shepherd should be shown in his whole attitude and expression. He is always ready for action. His athletic body looks full of explosive forces which he finds difficult to contain. The sparkling eyes, frank, eloquent with fire and flames in Belgian Shepherds full of temperament, are characteristic. They persuade us of their strength, their intrepidity and their readiness to pass into action. All this attitude of body and the specific expression of the head and eyes are very typical of the breed.'

His willingness to learn and to please is proverbial. Since a young puppy is already full of energy and curiosity, you have to

World Champion (1998) Sherpa van de Hoge Laer (Lupus van de Hoge Laer X G'Silence du Sart des Bois). Photo by Riitta Tjörneryd.

pay much attention to your Belgian Shepherd. Train him daily in basic obedience, in a brief training session, so that he is under control at all times.

Remember that boredom is the most frequent cause of problems. Boredom can be the cause of compulsive behaviours, such as stone chewing, continuous licking, tail chasing, constant barking, etc. He should never be bored, otherwise he will look for work himself, an occupational pastime that could be very unpleasant or irritating for you.

Walk your dog once a day on a long lead of 3 to 4 metres or a flexible lead that allows him even more freedom. If possible, find a suitable enclosed field where you can allow your Belgian Shepherd to run off-lead. Always keep his safety in mind. Go to different places; your dog will enjoy the

Ch Tee van de Hoge Laer (Glam du Sart des Bois X Kleo van de Hoge Laer). Photo by Riitta Tjörneryd.

and competitions, such as obedience training, agility, flyball, ring sport, guard or defence programmes, tracking, herding, etc. He is highly appreciated as a police or service dog and has proven his utility as a guide dog for the blind and as a Red Cross, customs, border patrol, avalanche, disaster or rescue dog. In the so-called ring sport competition, the Malinois really dominates the field.

In the sport of Schutzhund (defence dog) and International Working Regulations (IPO, *Internationale Prüfungsordnung*, the slightly different international form of Schutzhund), the Belgian Shepherd is very successful, in the US as well as in Europe. However, these disciplines, which include tracking, obedience and protection or defence work, are controversial in most English-speaking countries because, during the defence exercises, the dogs are taught to attack the

outing and the added stimulation of exploring 'uncharted territories.'

Because all dogs need companionship, many owners of Belgian Shepherds consider getting a second dog. This companion can be a smaller one, such as a Schipperke, which also is a Belgian herding dog with the typical Belgian temperament.

The character of the Belgian Shepherd can be considered to be a great virtue but, at the same time, it also comes with drawbacks.

First, let us look at the really positive and exceptional qualities of character, which have made him so popular as a working and guard dog. These qualities are his need for physical activity, his mental alertness, his intelligence, his willingness to please and his attachment and devotion to his master or mistress. These character traits make him highly trainable and able to excel in many programmes, disciplines

'criminal' (defence work assistant in complete defence outfit, with padded armguard and soft stick).

In the US the two dog breeds that predominate as 'dual-purpose' dogs to detect narcotics and to protect themselves and their handler are the Malinois and the ubiquitous German Shepherd.

The drawbacks of the Belgian Shepherd's character are related to his strong emotion and affection for his master. A Belgian Shepherd possesses neither the independent and hard character of the terriers nor the imperturbable behaviour of mountain or mastiff-type dogs. His unceasing devotion to his master, especially as a puppy, sometimes makes him 'emotionally needy,' excessively attention-seeking and even 'clingy.' Some owners of Belgian Shepherds find such behaviour very charming and cute and not unpleasant at all. However, if you regard this type of behaviour as undesirable, you can prevent or

Laekenois male and female: Upsilon and Ushuaïa des Fauves de Saline (Ch Opium van Kriekebos X Pastille van Kriekebos). Photo by Riitta Tjörneryd.

cure it with gentle but consistent training. Avoid being overly protective and ignore your dog when he exhibits excessively demanding behaviour, such as pawing, whimpering or licking. You should educate your dog with gentleness and firmness at the same time, avoiding any kind of harshness. A Belgian Shepherd, especially as a puppy, is very sensitive to his master's moods and his manner and tone of voice. When you are pleased with his behaviour, words of approval should always be his reward.

The Belgian Shepherd Dog can certainly be described as hypersensitive, impulsive and impetuous, sometimes mistakenly interpreted as 'nervous.' This term, however, sounds pejorative, suggesting a mental disorder. A Belgian Shepherd is not nervous; he is better described as active and full of spirit.

Sometimes his extremely fast reflexes have to be controlled lest they be perceived as too abrupt. The Belgian Shepherd

Groenendael male and female: Boris de la Pouroffe (Yako de la Pouroffe X Vallia des Forges Monceux) and Zette de la Pouroffe (Youpy de la Baraque de Planches X Yra des Forges Monceux). Photo by R Pollet.

The four varieties of Belgian Shepherd. Photo by Riitta Tjörneryd.

The four varieties on a painting (1987) by A Ackaert.

breed that is characterised as hypersensitive and very active. This behaviour can take the form of circling, excessive barking and chasing animals or anything that moves quickly. However, we have to stress that such behaviour results from innate aptitudes that have not been transformed into desirable behaviour by training. So it is well known that the Belgian Shepherd has a tendency to move in circles, which not only is due to his exuberant temperament but also results from his herding instinct, an inherited ability to guard and drive flocks. Today he still has the instinct to gather in a circle or to encircle all that is important to him: his flock, his family, his master during a walk, etc.

Barking also is a natural reaction of a watchful dog guarding his owner's property, home, car, sheep, etc. When your dog barks for hours when left alone in the house, the reason for this is loneliness. Nevertheless, it is a vice that can and must be

accomplishes every task at once, impetuously and swiftly. If you think that such a dog would exhaust you, we advise you to choose a dog of a more quiet or placid nature, not a Belgian Shepherd. Nevertheless, as to the character and temperament, great individual differences are possible, even within the same breed. Moreover, behavioural traits are always modified by training and experience.

Sometimes, Belgian Shepherds can be excitable. This again can be seen as almost normal and understandable in a

stopped by appropriate training.

Excitable behaviour in general can be cured by the owner always trying to remain calm and quiet, by giving the dog plenty of exercise and by avoiding any activities which trigger excitable behaviour.

PET QUALITIES

If you are an experienced dog trainer and purchase a Belgian Shepherd Dog, it goes without saying that you are making an excellent choice. You can go far with your talented Belgian Shepherd Dog, who thrives on challenges and proper training. We know that today only a few Belgian Shepherds are used for herding, but they surely belong to the most versatile of all breeds. Belgian Shepherds can be trained to high standards in all kinds of competitive disciplines, such as obedience, agility, tracking, and ring sport, and in all kinds of working trials, performance tests and related activities.

Besides dog training, dog shows also have become increasingly popular with Belgian Shepherd owners. However, when you want to show, you have to know that your dog can only reach the top placings when it is in a good condition and when it displays the desired physical and mental characteristics to a high degree. Taking part in a dog show

Three Malinois heads (Kennel van Bouwelhei). Photo by Riitta Tjörneryd.

beautiful Belgian Shepherds rightly feel proud and want to display this enthusiasm publicly. No specialised skills are required to show the dog but the dog must be in good condition, possess a well-kept coat and not be shy, aggressive or nervous. Training is of paramount importance, because judges will not tolerate unruly exhibits (nor should they have to). Visit a dog show to learn the protocol and meet the exhibitors. Before entering your dog, you are well advised to give your dog a little show training to teach him proper ring manners. Perhaps you would like to enter the dog in a ring craft class, which would be helpful even if you don't pursue the show ring seriously. You should also study the breed standard of the Belgian Shepherd so that you understand what the judges are looking for in a 'perfect specimen.'

can be exciting, but when your dog is not successful you can feel deeply disillusioned. Showing is not a sport for every owner, and, if at all possible, a new owner must decide whether or not he intends to show his puppy before purchasing him. A breeder who knows you intend to show will sell you a puppy that promises to be conformationally correct. Frequently, pet puppies have minor faults that, while not affecting their ability to be ideal pets, deem them less desirable for the show ring.

Many proud owners would very often like to show their Belgian Shepherds. This is only natural because owners of

Kouros of the Two (Grimm van de Hoge Laer X Glimpi of the Two).

If you are not interested in dog showing (or specialised advanced training or trials), you can still consider a Belgian Shepherd as a good breed choice for a pet and family dog. The great majority of Belgian Shepherds are kept simply as pets and the breed certainly offers many lovely pet dog qualities. It must be mentioned here that even a pet dog needs basic training to make him a suitable home companion.

Among the qualities that a Belgian Shepherd Dog possesses to make him a satisfying companion and family member include:

- sound health and low incidence of medical problems;
- affectionate behaviour, loyal dedication to his owner and his willingness to please;
- his obedience, responding well to commands and complying with basic house rules;
- protective and alert nature,

which makes him an ideal guard dog of your home and property;
- need for physical and mental activity, which will make him an excellent playmate and an ideal companion when you walk or train him;
- physical beauty, which will make him a pleasure to behold.

The Belgian Shepherds have the reputation of being good family dogs. They are beautiful, lively, affectionate, intelligent, trainable, adaptable and protective. All these attributes ensure their continued progress and ever-increasing popularity for showing, for participation in many canine sports and specialised training or working, and of course for selection as loyal and beautiful pets. More important than his obedience, intellect and service to

Grimm van de Hoge Laer (Zarka of the Two X Glimpi of the Two).

Belgian Shepherds and Schipperkes have a common ancestor called the Leuvenaar, which means inhabitant of Louvain, the well-known university city. Photo by R Pollet.

37

man is the Belgian Shepherd's loyalty. When you give him the proper care and love, your Belgian Shepherd will give you the devotion, immense love and fidelity that have made him famous throughout the world.

HEREDITARY PROBLEMS

The Belgian Shepherd Dog is a healthy dog. In many breeds, certain anatomical characteristics, which in the standards are described as typical and desirable, are so extreme that the dogs suffer from resulting unpleasant defects, such as breathing problems, eye irritations, skin infections, etc. The conformation and characteristics of the Belgian Shepherd Dog must be considered normal and not harmful to his health or well-being. This can be explained because, for example, he is not over- or undersized, his muzzle is not short, his skull not too broad or too narrow, his skin not too loose or too wrinkled, his body not overloaded, his joints not too straight or overangulated, etc. Fortunately, the Belgian Shepherd is not exaggerated in any way.

However, in dogs, many disorders are not directly related to the physical traits of a breed, but are inherited and entered into certain bloodlines by irresponsible or careless breeding. Fortunately we can assert that, although some common hereditary diseases indeed do occur in the Belgian Shepherd, they certainly do not

Whatever the colour or coat variety, all Belgian Shepherd Dogs have the same basic characteristics.

DO YOU KNOW ABOUT HIP DYSPLASIA?

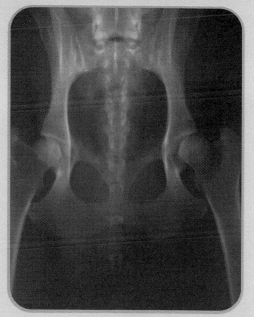

X-ray of a dog with 'good' hips.

X-ray of a dog with 'Moderate' dysplastic hips.

Hip dysplasia is a fairly common condition found in purebred dogs. When a dog has hip dysplasia, its hind leg has an incorrectly formed hip joint. By constant use of the hip joint, it becomes more and more loose, wears abnormally and may become arthritic.

Hip dysplasia can only be confirmed with an x-ray, but certain symptoms may indicate a problem. Your dog may have a hip dysplasia problem if it walks in a peculiar manner, hops instead of smoothly runs, uses his hind legs in unison (to keep the pressure off the weak joint), has trouble getting up from a prone position or always sits with both legs together on one side of its body.

As the dog matures, it may adapt well to life with a bad hip, but in a few years the arthritis develops and many dogs with hip dysplasia become cripples.

Hip dysplasia is considered an inherited disease and only can be diagnosed definitively when the dog is two years old. Some experts claim that a special diet might help your puppy outgrow the bad hip, but the usual treatments are surgical. The removal of the pectineus muscle, the removal of the round part of the femur, reconstructing the pelvis and replacing the hip with an artificial one are all surgical interventions that are expensive, but they are usually very successful. Follow the advice of your veterinary surgeon.

endanger the breed as a whole. Some of these hereditary disorders are briefly described here.

Hip Dysplasia (HD)

Hip dysplasia has the highest profile of all canine health problems and is the most widely discussed affliction in almost every breed of dog. Hip dysplasia simply means a malformed hip joint. The hip is a ball-and-socket joint. In normal hips the head (ball) of the femur fits solidly in the well-developed acetabulum (socket) of the hip bone. On x-rays of dogs with severe hip dysplasia, an abnormally shallow acetabulum and a small, misshapen or flattened femoral head can be seen. The differing degrees of shallow acetabulum, flattening of the femoral head and looseness at the hip joint are mostly rated as follows: A, no signs; B, transitional or near normal; C, mild; D, moderate; E, severe hip dysplasia.

The disease is of genetic origin, but nutritional and environmental factors also play a part. The breeders should avoid overfeeding their puppies, and, similarly, excessive exercise for puppies is not advisable.

Hip dysplasia occurs primarily in larger breeds and is less common in smaller breeds. The percentage of Belgian Shepherd Dogs being free from HD is rather high. Nevertheless, all Belgian Shepherd Dogs used for breeding should be certified free of HD. Breeding without HD control can be very detrimental to an expanding breed such as the Belgian Shepherd. Fortunately, in many countries, the clubs keep a hip x-ray registry and advise or require that Belgian Shepherds used for breeding have been x-rayed with negative results.

According to statistics of the x-ray examinations in France, more than 90 percent of the Belgian Shepherds are completely free (HD-0) or almost normal (transitional or HD-1). These results are considered to be reassuring, but they also present arguments to remain very vigilant.

The fact that hip dysplasia is less common in Belgian Shepherds than in many other Pastoral dogs is mostly attributable to the not-too-pronounced angulation in the hindlegs and the rather elegant structure and light weight of the breed with respect to size. The German Shepherd, with its extreme hindleg angulation, is among the worst sufferers of HD. Moreover, statistics of the occurrence of hip dysplasia in Belgian Shepherds prove that slow but still positive progress is being made.

When symptoms are visible, they can vary from mild lameness to permanent crippling. However, HD often has no clinical or observable symptoms.

This Belgian Malinois, easily clearing the hurdles, participates in a working trial. Belgian Shepherd Dogs are extremely agile, intelligent and trainable.

Many dogs that show no signs of suffering and move perfectly may still turn out to be affected after the x-rays have been reviewed. Dogs apparently are able to manage their dysplasia unless it becomes severe.

Some other hereditary disorders have also been diagnosed in the breed, but always only in a few number of dogs and in some breeding lines.

41

PROGRESSIVE RETINAL ATROPHY (PRA) AND CATARACTS

Several cases of progressive retinal atrophy (PRA), known as 'night blindness,' have been found in Belgian Shepherds in some countries. PRA is a degenerative condition involving the retina (the light-sensitive membrane at the back of the eyeball). Night blindness is an early clinical sign, leading to a progressive loss of vision and eventual total blindness. Unfortunately, no effective treatment exists. Elimination of the disease is only possible by avoiding affected animals in breeding programmes. The problem, however, is that it usually becomes apparent only in older dogs, which makes it difficult to eradicate.

Cataracts, both juvenile and adult, have also been experienced in some breeding lines. Cataracts can be defined as an inherited tendency to opacity of the eye lens, which can progress to complete blindness. Fortunately, more and more breeders are checking and certifying breeding stock for all eye problems.

EPILEPSY

Epilepsy, an inherited disease in which there are spasmodic fits, has become fairly widespread in the long-haired Belgian Shepherd varieties. The mode of inheritance is complex. Treatment with oral anti-epileptic drugs is possible. However, seizures can be so frequent that coma and death may occur.

Epilepsy in the Belgian Shepherd Dog is now an acknowledged serious problem, though many breeders in the past were reluctant to discuss it. At the moment, in some countries, research projects have been started to examine heritability and to survey how widespread the problem is. Moreover, many clubs require that breeding stock is screened free of epilepsy.

The Belgian Shepherd Dog has always been a relatively healthy breed. He requires no special care and has a low incidence of medical problems. He is likely, when properly cared for, to go through life never needing the services of a veterinary surgeon apart from routine visits. It is most likely that your dog will never suffer from any of these hereditary defects. Nevertheless, breeding committees of the Belgian Shepherd clubs all over the world, which are dedicated to the welfare of the breed, must remain vigilant to avoid breed-specific problems or hereditary disorders. These problems can, as has been seen in many other breeds, become rapidly widespread and common, when no health tests for breeding are required.

The Breed Standard for the
BELGIAN SHEPHERD DOG

Every owner of a Belgian Shepherd Dog asks himself the question one day: 'What does the perfect Belgian Shepherd Dog look like?' or 'What is the value of my dog as a representative of its breed?'

To find the answer, it should be enough to read the breed standard and thereby determine how well your dog measures up. However, for the novice, who has not yet acquired sufficient knowledge of canine structure and canine terminology, the breed standard is not an adequate guide.

A breed standard is used by the governing kennel clubs to describe the ideal or 'model dog'

The standard by which Belgian Shepherd Dogs are judged and bred enables them to retain their physical characteristics. This young Groenendael has a remarkable coat.

of each recognised breed. Show dogs are judged against this standard, which describes the ideal physical and temperamental characteristics of the perfect specimen.

Many of those interested in the Belgian Shepherd Dog are inclined to think that the German Shepherd Dog and the Belgian Shepherd Dog are very similar. Even today, in articles and books on shepherd dogs, we can read that the Belgian Shepherd Dog is smaller in size, which is false, and weighs less, which is true. That its shape would be 'rather similar to that of the German Shepherd' is a completely false statement, since the type and the silhouette of these two breeds are completely different.

Nevertheless, in 1897 the Count de Bylandt wrote that the German, Belgian and Dutch Shepherds belonged to one breed only, which should be named the 'Continental Shepherd.' When we look at photographs of dogs of 70 to 80 years ago, we have to admit that the likeness shared by these three breeds was great. However, their appearances have changed enormously since then. The German Shepherd especially has changed very strongly in type, even since World War II. This is less the case with the Belgian Shepherd. In fact, the type, meaning the general outline or appearance, has not changed fundamentally in the last few decades.

When comparing the Belgian Shepherd to the German Shepherd, the distinguishing features of the Belgian Shepherd are:

- a lighter skeleton, more elegant appearance and the high carriage of the head;
- the impression of refinement of the 'finely chiselled' head, which means that the head should not be coarse or heavy, but dry, with close-fitting, not slack or wrinkled, skin, and with clean-cut lines and contours;
- that it is a square dog, he is not longer than tall; the body, from the front of the chest to the back of the buttocks, fits into a square, not into a rectangle;
- the angulations (the angles formed at the joints by the meeting of the bones) are moderate to normal, not excessive as in many German Shepherds (especially American ones); consequently, the hind legs are well under the body when the dog is standing or in 'show stance';
- the rather short length of reach or the short strides (the distance covered with each stride) when trotting; this is a consequence of the square body structure and the moderate angulation of the fore and the hindquarters.

When comparing the English Kennel Club breed standard to the official standard on the Continent (the FCI standard), no significant differences can be seen, except the description of the colour of the Tervueren and the Malinois. According to The Kennel Club standard, grey is a fully accepted colour in the Tervueren and the Malinois. The FCI standard, however, states that (1) in the Tervueren, the fawn colour with black overlay and black mask (black muzzle) is the preferred one; (2) in the Malinois, only the fawn colour with black overlay and black mask is acceptable; and (3) in both the Tervueren and Malinois, grey is not desirable. The Groenendael is only solid black and the Laekenois only fawn with traces of black overlay.

In the United States, the American Kennel Club (AKC) recognises the Belgian Sheepdog (Groenendael), the Belgian Tervuren and the Belgian Malinois

as three separate breeds and thus publishes three official standards. The Laekenois is denied registration with the AKC. When comparing the American to the FCI standard, there are no fundamental differences and the description of the colours is very similar. So we can read in the American standard that the colour of the Belgian Tervuren should be 'rich fawn to russet mahogany with black overlay' and that 'washed out predominant color, such as cream or gray, is to be severely penalized.' In the Malinois 'the basic coloring is rich fawn to mahogany, with black tips on the hairs giving an overlay appearance,' and no other allowed colour is mentioned. The British standard also includes 'grey with black overlay' in its description of the desirable colours for the Tervueren and Malinois.

According to all the standards,

The main similarity between the German Shepherd Dog, shown here at a demonstration at a British dog show, and the Belgian Shepherd Dog is their suitability for police and military work. Conformationally, these two breeds are vastly different.

the desired characteristics of the Belgian Shepherd, without comment on the coat or colour, could read as follows: 'an elegant square body; head long, wedge shaped, finely chiselled and carried highly; dark, almond-shaped eyes, lively look; small, triangular, stiff upstanding ears; horizontal backline; croup only very slightly inclined; chest well let down, but upwards curving abdomen's underline; sufficient angulations; movement firm and supple, with moderate stride; a sparkling temperament and a character assured, without fear whatsoever nor aggressiveness.'

It is important, for the preservation of the breed and its international esteem, that there be a unified type all over the world. During the last decades in the UK and Scandinavian countries there has been a progressive evolution towards the elegant type, square body and finely chiselled heads, as specified and desired in the country of origin. However, it is a pity that in the United States still too many, even Best in Show-winning, Belgian Shepherds are lacking elegance and are too long in body, with too heavy bone and overly pronounced angulation. This is rather surprising because we can read in the three American standards that a Belgian is 'elegant in appearance' and that the body is 'square' ('the length equal to the height') and the head 'clean-cut' or 'well chiselled' ('with clean outline').

We have to warn also about a possible divergence of the type into four different appearances. In *The Blueprint of the Belgian Shepherd Dog*, written by this author, it states: 'Although the coats and colour differentiate the varieties, it is well known that the danger exists that the four varieties would develop into different types. It would be a very bad thing for the Belgian Shepherd if the four varieties had already developed so much that there would be in reality four types, and that going back to the original type would not be possible anymore.'

In Belgium and in many other countries, it is possible, in order to

The eyes should be medium size, preferably dark brown with black-rimmed eyelids.

ensure that the type does not diverge, to obtain permission for inter-variety breeding, when the request from the breeder is supported by serious and strong arguments. Therefore, in FCI countries and the UK, a long-haired fawn (Tervueren) puppy, bred from Groenendael parents, should be registered as a Tervueren and not as a 'red Groenendael.'

THE KENNEL CLUB STANDARD FOR THE BELGIAN SHEPHERD DOG

General Appearance: Medium-sized dog, well proportioned, intelligent, attentive, hardy and alert [Four Varieties: Groenendael, Laekenois, Malinois and Tervueren.]

Characteristics: With fine proportions and proud carriage of head, conveying an impression of graceful strength. Not only a sheep dog, but a guard dog.

Temperament: Wary, neither timid, nervous nor aggressive.

Head and Skull: Head finely chiselled, long but not excessively so. Skull and muzzle roughly equal in length, with at most slight bias in favour of muzzle, giving impression of a balanced whole. Skull of medium width in proportion to length of head, forehead flat, centre line

The head should be finely chiselled and long, but not excessively so.

not very pronounced; in profile, parallel to imaginary line extending muzzle line. Muzzle of medium length tapering gradually to nose. Nose black, well-flared nostrils. Moderate stop. Arches above eyes not prominent, muzzle finely chiselled under eyes. Cheeks spare, quite flat but well muscled.

Eyes: Medium size, neither protruding nor sunken, slightly almond-shaped, preferably dark brown; black rimmed eyelids. Direct, lively and enquiring look.

Ears: Distinctly triangular appearance, stiff and erect, set high, moderate length with external ear well rounded at base.

The Belgian Shepherd Dog's body should be powerful but elegant.

Mouth: Wide, lips thin-textured, very firm, strongly pigmented. Strong white teeth firmly set in well developed jaws. Scissor bite, i.e. upper teeth closely overlapping lower teeth and set square to the jaws. Pincer bite tolerated.

Neck: Very supple. Neck slightly elongated, well muscled and without dewlap, broadening slightly towards shoulders. Nape very slightly arched.

Forequarters: Withers distinct, strongly boned throughout with wiry, powerful muscle structure. Shoulder blades long and oblique, firmly attached, flat, forming such angle with humerus as to enable elbows to work easily. Forelegs long, well muscled, parallel. Pasterns strong and short. Carpus clearly defined. Dewclaws permissible.

Body: Body powerful but elegant. In males, length from point of shoulders to point of buttocks approximately equal to height at withers. In females slightly longer

Correct body structure: strong, straight back; deep chest; no excessive tuck-up.

Weak back with curving topline, chest not well developed, excessive tuck-up.

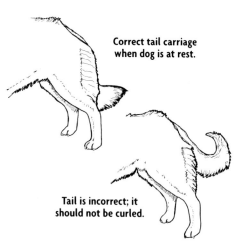

Correct tail carriage when dog is at rest.

Tail is incorrect; it should not be curled.

Ears should be triangular and set high on head.

Ears set too far apart.

Correct hindquarters; legs parallel when viewed from behind.

Weak hindquarters; legs and feet turning out.

Forelegs are long and straight, parallel when viewed from front.

Incorrect forequarters; legs too close together and feet turning out.

The Groenendael variety has an outer coat that is long, straight and abundant.

permissible. Chest deep and well let down. Ribs moderately well sprung. Upper line of body straight, broad and powerfully muscled. Belly moderately developed neither drooping nor unduly cut up continuing lower line of chest in a graceful curve. Rump very slightly sloping, broad but not excessively so. Skin springy but quite taut over whole body. All external mucous membranes highly pigmented.

Hindquarters: Well muscled and powerful. Good but not excessive angulation; hocks well let down. Viewed from behind, legs parallel. Dewclaws to be removed.

Feet: Toes arched, very close together; soles thick and springy with large dark claws. Forefeet round. Hindfeet slightly oval.

Tail: Firmly set, strong at base, of medium length. When at rest, hangs down, with tip slightly bent backwards at level of hock; when moving it should lift accentuating curve towards tip, never curled, nor bent to one side. Tip may be carried slightly higher than topline.

Gait/Movement: Brisk, free and even.

Coat: There are three distinctive coat types:

Groenendael/Tervueren
Outer coat long, straight and abundant. Texture of medium harshness. Not silky or wiry. Undercoat extremely dense. Hair shorter on head, outside of ears and lower part of legs. Opening of ear protected by hair. Hair especially long and abundant, ruff-like around neck, particularly in males. Fringe of long hair down back of forelegs, long and abundant hair evident on hindquarters and tail. Males longer coated than females.

Laekenois
Harsh, wiry, dry and not curly. Any sprinkling of fluffy fine hair in locks in rough coats is undesirable. Length of coat about 6 cms (2.5 ins) on all parts of body. Hair around eyes but not to obscure them. Muzzle hair not so long as to make head appear square or heavy. Tail not plumed.

Malinois
Hair very short on head, exterior of

ears and lower parts of legs. Short on rest of body, thicker on tail and around neck where it resembles a ridge or collar, beginning at base of ear and extending to throat. Hindquarters fringed with longer hair. Tail thick and bushy. Coat thick, close of good firm texture with woolly undercoat, neither silky nor wiry.

NO VARIATION IN THESE TYPES IS ACCEPTABLE.

Colour: The acceptable colours relate directly to coat type.

Groenendael
Black or black with limited white as follows: small to moderate patch or strip on chest, between pads of feet and on tips of hind toes. Frosting (white or grey) on muzzle.

Laekenois
Reddish fawn with black shading, principally in muzzle and tail.

Tervueren/Malinois
All shades of red, fawn, grey with black overlay. Coat characteristically double pigmented, wherein tip of each light coloured hair is blacked. On mature males this blackening especially pronounced on shoulders, back and rib sections. Black mask on face, not extended above line of eyes and ears mostly black. Tail should have a darker or black tip. Small to moderate white patch or strip permitted on chest, between pads of feet and on tips of hind toes. Frosting (white or grey) on muzzle. Beyond the age of 18 months a washed out colour or colour too black undesirable.

NO VARIATION ON THESE COLOURS BY COAT TYPE IS ACCEPTABLE.

Size: Ideal height: dogs: 61–66 cms (24–26 ins); bitches: 56–61 cms (22–24 ins). Weight, in proportion to size.

Faults: Any departure from the foregoing points should be considered a fault and the seriousness with which the fault should be regarded should be in exact proportion to its degree.

Note: Male animals should have two apparently normal testicles fully descended into the scrotum.

Despite their rather different appearances, the Belgian Shepherds are structurally identical except for coat and colour.

Nothing is more exciting than selecting a Belgian Shepherd puppy. When you and your family have decided that a Belgian Shepherd Dog is really the most suitable dog for you, you can locate a recommended kennel and make a careful choice.

Before you talk to a breeder, you have to know what you intend to do with your new companion. He should fit in your daily routine, now and in the years to come. Will you show your new Belgian Shepherd or enter him in working or herding trials or do you simply desire a pet?

The responsibilities you will have and the consequences of keeping a dog should be considered before you choose and visit a breeder, as your dog will rely completely on you.

You have to realise that:

- All family members should be enthusiastic about acquiring a puppy.
- Your children should regard the dog, under your supervision, as a playmate, not a plaything, and they should be capable of respecting the dog. They should also be instructed in how to handle him properly.
- Taking care of a dog—feeding him, walking him, educating him, grooming him, looking after him for a lifetime—will be a time-consuming commitment.
- Food, veterinary bills, etc., must be included in the family budget.

'YOU BETTER SHOP AROUND!'

Finding a reputable breeder that sells healthy pups is very important, but make sure that the breeder you choose is not only someone you respect but also with whom you feel comfortable. Your breeder will be a resource long after you buy your puppy, and you must be able to call with reasonable questions without being made to feel like a pest! If you don't connect on a personal level, investigate some other breeders before making a final decision.

• When you go away on holiday, you have to take him with you or somebody has to look after him.

ACQUIRING A PUPPY

If all these requirements do not present a problem, you can choose a reputable breeder and kennel, but do not act impulsively. Do not let your choice of a kennel be determined by its nearness to your home and do not buy the first puppy that licks your nose.

Advice on buying a Belgian Shepherd puppy can be given by a veterinary surgeon or you can enquire at a local dog-training club. The best way to find a reputable seller, however, is to contact committee members of the breed club.

A caring, responsible breeder raises his litters in his home. When viewing a litter, he will give you good advice and assistance, but help him by stating, as precisely as possible, the sort of puppy you want (dog or bitch) and the purpose for which you desire it, as a family pet or for showing, breeding, training, working, etc.

A good kennel consistently produces healthy and sound dogs and also provides good after-sales service. In any case, avoid puppy farms or mills.

A responsible breeder will show you the mother and also

PREPARING FOR A PUP

Unfortunately, when a puppy is bought by someone who does not take into consideration the time and attention that dog ownership requires, it is the puppy who suffers when he is either abandoned or placed in a shelter by a frustrated owner. So all of the 'homework' you do in preparation for your pup's arrival will benefit you both. The more informed you are, the more you will know what to expect and the better equipped you will be to handle the ups and downs of raising a puppy. Hopefully, everyone in the household is willing to do his part in raising and caring for the pup. The anticipation of owning a dog often brings a lot of promises from excited family members: 'I will walk him every day,' 'I will feed him,' 'I will housebreak him,' etc., but these things take time and effort, and promises can easily be forgotten once the novelty of the new pet has worn off.

the father if available. Their appearance and behaviour will give you some idea of your puppy's mature appearance and temperament. The breeder will also explain to you how a pedigree is read and inform you about the 'bloodlines' and the merits of the parents and grandparents. Do not underestimate the importance of their character and anatomical structure if you wish your puppy to grow up to be a high-quality adult Belgian Shepherd Dog. However, you need to be lucky too. You have to realise

PUPPY SELECTION

Your selection of a good puppy can be determined by your needs. A show potential or a good pet? It is your choice. Every puppy, however, should be of good temperament. Although show-quality puppies are bred and raised with emphasis on physical conformation, responsible breeders strive for equally good temperament. Do not buy from a breeder who concentrates solely on physical beauty at the expense of personality.

that you are fortunate when you can make your puppy, coming from 'champion lines,' a champion, but a champion, coming from parents of inferior value, would be a miracle!

Watch the behaviour of the puppies together in the litter. Do

If at all possible, ask to view the parent(s) of your potential puppy. Keep in mind that the dam may look a tad under the weather, given her strenuous weeks of labour and puppy rearing.

INSURANCE

Many good breeders will offer you insurance with your new puppy, which is an excellent idea. The first few weeks of insurance will probably be covered free of charge or with only minimal cost, allowing you to take up the policy when this expires. If you own a pet dog, it is sensible to take out such a policy as veterinary fees can be high, although routine vaccinations and boosters are not covered. Look carefully at the many options open to you before deciding which suits you best.

not choose a shy or retiring puppy, which may grow to be insecure or fearful, a possible occurrence in Belgian Shepherds. On the other hand, very assertive puppies can develop into overly dominant adults. Try to select an outgoing, confident and alert puppy who seems bright and looks healthy and who is willing to play and comes running towards you. A puppy should not be fearful about normal noises. He should

DID YOU KNOW?
You should not even think about buying a puppy that looks sick, undernourished, overly frightened or nervous. Sometimes a timid puppy will warm up to you after a 30-minute 'let's-get-acquainted' session.

DOCUMENTATION

Two important documents you will get from the breeder are the pup's pedigree and registration certificate. The breeder should register the litter and each pup with The Kennel Club, and it is necessary for you to have the paperwork if you plan on showing or breeding in the future.

Make sure you know the breeder's intentions on which type of registration he will obtain for the pup. There are limited registrations which may prohibit the dog from being shown, bred or from competing in non-conformation trials such as Working or Agility if the breeder feels that the pup is not of sufficient quality to do so. There is also a type of registration that will permit the dog in non-conformation competition only.

On the reverse side of the registration certificate, the new owner can find the transfer section which must be signed by the breeder.

not hide but rather show interest when you drop a metal object like a key or hit a metal pan with a spoon. You should not buy any puppy of the litter, even one that seems to behave normally, if most of them show fear or cannot be approached. Ideally, when entering the room with the litter, the pups should all approach you, jump on you and compete for attention. An extroverted character will be an advantage, for training as well as showing. Take into consideration, though, that pups sleep as much as 18 hours a day and that your visit might coincide with one of their many naps!

It is rather difficult, if you want to buy a show-quality Belgian Shepherd, for this author to offer advice on the structure and conformation. An experienced breeder should be able to guide you in your choice of a puppy, especially as early as six to eight weeks. There are very few persons who are experts in Belgian Shepherds, and even experts can be mistaken.

A good Belgian Shepherd puppy should have a firm and square body; the back or topline should already be firm and horizontal, with no dip or roach (arching); the legs, both front and rear, straight and parallel to each other, not bowed and not placed too close together (without a cowhock look); the ears as small as possible and between 7 and 12 weeks already firmly upright.

Choose a pup that, rather than hopping, already is able to trot easily, with a parallel movement of the fore and the hindquarters, while the topline remains firm and level.

A potbelly is a possible sign of worms. Anyway, ask the breeder whether the pups have been wormed, inoculated, etc.

Coat colour is important in the Belgian Shepherd. The amount of black overlay that a Tervueren or Malinois will have when mature is not easily predictable, but is often evident shortly after birth. In these two varieties, you have to look for an overall warm fawn-based colour, which can be seen from about seven weeks. The black overlay then develops again at that time. At any age, the dark muzzle or mask should always be pronounced.

Any white should be avoided in the Tervueren, the Malinois, the wholly black Groenendael and the fawn Laekenois, except when at most confined to the toes and a small patch on the forechest.

Decide which sex you prefer. There are some specific differences. Males are physically more impressive. They carry more coat, especially the long-haired, and generally have a major shedding about once a year. They have a greater tendency to be independent and to wander further afield. They are more pugnacious and sometimes aggressive to other males. They mark their territory in a demonstrative manner.

Bitches are more feminine, smaller and less powerfully built. Normally they come into season every 6 months for 21 days. At the beginning, the heat is marked with a clear mucous-like discharge from the vagina. Very often, however, the bitch's

All puppies are adorable and all attract children's love and attention...for a short time. Bringing any dog into your home requires a great deal of soul-searching. Are you ready for the expense in terms of time and money?

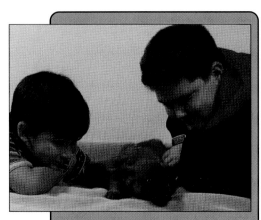

PUPPY PERSONALITY

When a litter becomes available to you, choosing a pup out of all those adorable faces will not be an easy task! Sound temperament is of utmost importance, but each pup has its own personality and some may be better suited to you than others. A feisty, independent pup will do well in a home with older children and adults, while quiet, shy puppies will thrive in a home with minimum noise and distractions. Your breeder knows the pups best and should be able to guide you in the right direction.

affectionate and also more submissive. Moreover, some people find that a bitch is easier to housetrain than a male.

Nevertheless, all of these sex differences should not be overemphasised. In fact, both sexes are highly trainable and remarkably dedicated to their owner.

The best age to bring a puppy home is between seven and eight weeks, certainly not older than nine. The reason is that during the so-called sociali-sation period (3 to 12 weeks), the pups should be handled by a wide variety of people, exposed to as many experiences as possible and have contact with other dogs, other animals and humans, without becoming stressed.

You should ask the breeder to show you the parents' registration documents, certifi-

frequent licking is noticed first. After about seven days, the discharge is bloody and can be copious; during the third week the discharge eases up. During the period of the season, you will have to keep your bitch away from male dogs in order to prevent unwanted matings. Bitches are generally more friendly, a little more

FEEDING TIP

You will probably start feeding your pup the same food that he has been getting from the breeder; the breeder should give you a few days' supply to start you off. Although you should not give your pup too many treats, you will want to have puppy treats on hand for coaxing, training, rewards, etc. Be careful, though, as a small pup's calorie requirements are relatively low and a few treats can add up to almost a full day's worth of calories without the required nutrition.

cates of performance (breed shows, temperament tests, obedience and working trials, etc.) and health certificates.

When you have made your purchase, a responsible and caring breeder will also give you a diet sheet and possibly some food for the first meals in the new home.

Like many purchasers you can keep in touch with the breeder for many years to come, but don't trouble him about insignificant problems!

COMMITMENT OF OWNERSHIP

After considering all of these factors, you have made some very important decisions about selecting your puppy. If you have selected a breeder, you have gone a step further—you have made valuable contacts and located a responsible, conscientious person who breeds healthy and sound Belgian Shepherds. If you have observed a litter in action, you have obtained a

QUALITY FOOD

The cost of food must also be mentioned. All dogs need a good quality food with an adequate supply of protein to develop their bones and muscles properly. Most dogs are not picky eaters but unless fed properly they can quickly succumb to skin problems.

PUPPY APPEARANCE

Your puppy should have a well-fed appearance but not a distended abdomen, which may indicate worms or incorrect feeding, or both. The body should be firm, with a solid feel. The skin of the abdomen should be pale pink and clean, without signs of scratching or rash. Check the hind legs to make certain that dewclaws were removed, if any were present at birth.

firsthand look at the dynamics of a puppy 'pack' and, thus, you should learn about each pup's individual personality—perhaps you have even found one that particularly appeals to you.

However, even if you have not yet found the Belgian Shepherd puppy of your dreams, observing pups will help you learn to recognise certain behaviour and to determine what a pup's behaviour indicates about his temperament. You will

The short-haired Malinois puppy will require the least grooming of the four Belgian Shepherds. For owners who dread dog hair about the house, the Malinois is the best choice.

59

be able to pick out which pups are the leaders, which ones are less outgoing, which ones are confident, which ones are shy, playful, friendly, aggressive, etc. Equally as important, you will learn to recognise what a healthy pup should look and act like. All of these things will help you in your search, and when you find the Belgian Shepherd that was meant for you, you will know it!

DO YOUR HOMEWORK!
In order to know whether or not a puppy will fit into your lifestyle, you need to assess his personality. A good way to do this is to interact with his parents. Your pup inherits not only his appearance but also his personality and temperament from the sire and dam. If the parents are fearful or overly aggressive, these same traits may likely show up in your puppy.

YOUR SCHEDULE...
If you lead an erratic, unpredictable life, with daily or weekly changes in your work requirements, consider the problems of owning a puppy. The new puppy has to be fed regularly, socialised (loved, petted, handled, introduced to other people) and, most importantly, allowed to visit outdoors for toilet training. As the dog gets older, it can be more tolerant of deviations in its feeding and toilet relief.

Researching your breed, selecting a responsible breeder and observing as many pups as possible are all important steps on the way to dog ownership. It may seem like a lot of effort... and you have not even taken the pup home yet! Remember, though, you cannot be too careful when it comes to deciding on the type of dog you want and finding out about your prospective pup's background. Buying a puppy is not—or should not be—just another whimsical purchase. This is one instance in which you actually do get to choose your own family! You may be thinking that buying a puppy should be fun— it should not be so serious and so much work. Keep in mind that your puppy is not a cuddly stuffed toy or decorative lawn ornament, but a creature that will become a real member of your family. You will come to realise that, while buying a puppy is a pleasurable and exciting endeavour, it is not something to be taken lightly. Relax…the fun will start when the pup comes home!

PREPARING PUPPY'S PLACE IN YOUR HOME

Researching your breed and finding a breeder are only two aspects of the 'homework' you will have to do before taking your Belgian Shepherd puppy home. You will also have to prepare your home and family for the new addition. Much as you would prepare a nursery for a newborn baby, you will need to designate a place in your home that will be the puppy's own. How you prepare your home will depend on how much freedom the dog will be allowed. Whatever you decide, you must ensure that he has a place that he can 'call his own.'

When you bring your new puppy into your home, you are bringing him into what will become his home as well. Obviously, you did not buy a puppy so that he could take over your house, but in order for a puppy to grow into a stable, well-adjusted dog, he has to feel comfortable in his surroundings. Remember, he is leaving the warmth and security of his

A FORTNIGHT'S GRACE
It will take at least two weeks for your puppy to become accustomed to his new surroundings. Give him lots of love, attention, handling, frequent opportunities to relieve himself, a diet he likes to eat and a place he can call his own.

mother and littermates, as well as the familiarity of the only place he has ever known, so it is important to make his transition as easy as possible. By preparing a place in your home for the puppy, you are making him feel as welcome as possible in a strange new place. It should not take him long to get used to it, but the sudden shock of being transplanted is somewhat traumatic for a young pup. Imagine how a small child would feel in the same situation—that is how your puppy must be feeling. It is up to you to reassure him and to let him know, 'Little chap, you are going to like it here!'

61

PHOTO COURTESY OF DOSKOCIL

recommending crates as preferred tools for show puppies as well as pet puppies. Crates are not cruel—crates have many humane and highly effective uses in dog care and training. For example, crate training is a very popular and very successful housebreaking method. A crate can keep your dog safe during travel and, perhaps most importantly, a crate provides your dog with a place of his own in your home. It serves as a 'doggie bedroom' of sorts—your Belgian Shepherd can curl up in his crate when he wants to sleep or when he just needs a break. Many dogs sleep in their crates overnight. With soft bedding and his favourite toy, a crate becomes a cosy pseudo-den for your dog. Like his ancestors, he too will seek out the comfort and retreat of a den—you just happen to be providing him with something a little more luxurious than what his early ancestors enjoyed.

As far as purchasing a crate, the type that you buy is up to you. It will most likely be one of the two most popular types: wire or fibreglass. There are advantages and disadvantages to each type. For example, a wire crate is more open, allowing the air to flow through and affording the dog a view of what is going on around him while a fibreglass crate is

Your local pet shop will have a large variety of crates from which you can choose the type that best suits your needs. Purchase a crate that is large enough for the fully grown dog.

WHAT YOU SHOULD BUY

CRATE
To someone unfamiliar with the use of crates in dog training, it may seem like punishment to shut a dog in a crate, but this is not the case at all. Although all breeders do not advocate crate training, more and more breeders and trainers are

sturdier. Both can double as travel crates, providing protection for the dog. The size of the crate is another thing to consider. Puppies do not stay puppies forever—in fact, sometimes it seems as if they grow right before your eyes. A small crate may be fine for a very young Belgian Shepherd pup, but it will not do him much good for long! Unless you have the money and the inclination to buy a new crate every time your pup has a growth spurt, it is better to get one that will accommodate your dog both as a pup and at full size. A medium-size crate will be necessary for a full-grown Belgian Shepherd, who stands approximately 66 cms (26 ins) high.

BEDDING

Veterinary bedding in the dog's crate will help the dog feel more at home and you may also like to pop in a small blanket. This will take the place of the leaves,

STRESS-FREE

Some experts in canine health advise that stress during a dog's early years of development can compromise and weaken his immune system and may trigger the potential for a shortened life expectancy. They emphasise the need for happy and stress-free growing-up years.

CRATE TRAINING TIPS

During crate training, you should partition off the section of the crate in which the pup stays. If he is given too big an area, this will hinder your training efforts. Crate training is based on the fact that a dog does not like to soil his sleeping quarters, so it is ineffective to keep a pup in a crate that is so big that he can eliminate in one end and get far enough away from it to sleep. Also, you want to make the crate den-like for the pup. Blankets and a favourite toy will make the crate cosy for the small pup; as he grows, you may want to evict some of his 'roommates' to make more room.

It will take some coaxing at first, but be patient. Given some time to get used to it, your pup will adapt to his new home-within-a-home quite nicely.

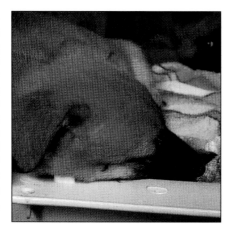

twigs, etc., that the pup would use in the wild to make a den; the pup can make his own 'burrow' in the crate. Although your pup is far removed from his den-making ancestors, the denning instinct is still a part of his genetic makeup. Second, until you take your pup home, he has been sleeping amidst the warmth of his mother and litter-mates, and while a blanket is not the same as a warm, breathing body, it still provides heat and something with which to snuggle. You will want to wash your pup's bedding frequently in case he has an accident in his crate, and replace or remove any blanket that becomes ragged and starts to fall apart.

Toys

Toys are a must for dogs of all ages, especially for curious playful pups. Puppies are the 'children' of the dog world, and

what child does not love toys? Chew toys provide enjoyment for both dog and owner—your dog will enjoy playing with his favourite toys, while you will enjoy the fact that they distract him from your expensive shoes and leather sofa. Puppies love to chew; in fact, chewing is a physical need for pups as they are teething, and everything looks appetising! The full range of your possessions—from old tea towel to Oriental carpet—are fair game in the eyes of a teething pup. Puppies are not all that discerning when it comes to

MENTAL AND DENTAL

Toys not only help your puppy get the physical and mental stimulation he needs but also provide a great way to keep his teeth clean. Hard rubber or nylon toys, especially those constructed with grooves, are designed to scrape away plaque, preventing bad breath and gum infection.

finding something to literally 'sink their teeth into'— everything tastes great!

Belgian Shepherd puppies are fairly aggressive chewers and only the hardest, strongest toys should be offered to them. Breeders advise owners to resist stuffed toys, because they can become de-stuffed in no time. The overly excited pup may ingest the stuffing, which is neither digestible nor nutritious.

Similarly, squeaky toys are quite popular, but must be avoided for the Belgian Shepherd. Perhaps a squeaky toy can be used as an aid in training, but not for free play. If a pup 'disembowels' one of these, the small plastic squeaker inside can be dangerous if swallowed. Monitor the condition of all your pup's toys carefully and get rid of any that have been chewed to

TOYS, TOYS, TOYS!

With a big variety of dog toys available, and so many that look like they would be a lot of fun for a dog, be careful in your selection. It is amazing what a set of puppy teeth can do to an innocent-looking toy, so, obviously, safety is a major consideration. Be sure to choose the most durable products that you can find. Hard nylon bones and toys are a safe bet, and many of them are offered in different scents and flavours that will be sure to capture your dog's attention. It is always fun to play a game of catch with your dog, and there are balls and flying discs that are specially made to withstand dog teeth.

Tug toys are popular with many dogs. Be wary of engaging in overly zealous contests with your dog.

the point of becoming potentially dangerous.

Be careful of natural bones, which have a tendency to splinter into sharp, dangerous

PLAY'S THE THING

Teaching the puppy to play with his toys in running and fetching games is an ideal way to help the puppy develop muscle, learn motor skills and bond with you his owner and master.

He also needs to learn how to inhibit his bite reflex and never to use his teeth on people, forbidden objects and other animals in play. Whenever you play with your puppy, you make the rules. This becomes an important message to your puppy in teaching him that you are the pack leader and control everything he does in life. Once your dog accepts you as his leader, your relationship with him will be cemented for life.

Your local pet shop will have a variety of leads that are suitable for puppies and adults. Purchase one that is 3 to 4 metres in length.

LEAD

A nylon lead is probably the best option as it is the most resistant to puppy teeth should your pup take a liking to chewing on his lead. Of course, this is a habit that should be nipped in the bud, but if your pup likes to chew on his lead he has a very slim chance of being able to chew through the strong nylon. Nylon leads are also lightweight, which is good for a young Belgian Shepherd who is just getting used to the idea of walking on a lead. For everyday walking and safety purposes, the nylon lead is a good choice. As your pup grows up and gets used to walking on the lead, you may want to purchase a flexible lead. These leads allow you to extend the length to give the dog

pieces. Also be careful of rawhide, which can turn into pieces that are easy to swallow and become a mushy mess on your carpet.

a broader area to explore or to shorten the length to keep the dog near you. Of course there are special leads for training purposes, and specially made leather harnesses, but these are not necessary for routine walks.

COLLAR

Your pup should get used to wearing a collar all the time since you will want to attach his ID tags to it. You have to attach the lead to something! A lightweight nylon collar is a good choice; make sure that it fits snugly enough so that the pup cannot wriggle out of it, but is loose enough so that it will not be uncomfortably tight around the pup's neck. You should be able to fit a finger between the pup and the collar. It may take some time for your pup to get used to wearing the collar, but soon he will not even notice that it is there. Choke collars are made for training, but should only be used by an experienced handler.

FOOD AND WATER BOWLS

Your pup will need two bowls, one for food and one for water. You may want two sets of bowls, one for inside and one for outside, depending on where the dog will be fed and where he will be spending time. Stainless steel or sturdy plastic bowls are popular choices. Plastic bowls

FINANCIAL RESPONSIBILITY
Grooming tools, collars, leashes, dog beds and, of course, toys will be an expense to you when you first obtain your pup, and the cost will continue throughout your dog's lifetime. If your puppy damages or destroys your possessions (as most puppies surely will!) or something belonging to a neighbour, you can calculate additional expense. There is also flea and pest control, which every dog owner faces more than once. You must be able to handle the financial responsibility of owning a dog.

are more chewable. Dogs tend not to chew on the steel variety, which can be sterilised. It is important to buy sturdy bowls since anything is in danger of being chewed by puppy teeth

Your local pet shop will have many different types of bowls made from heavy and light plastic, pottery and stainless steel.

It is your responsibility to clean up after your dog. Your local pet shop should have some devices that will make the job easier.

and you do not want your dog to be constantly chewing apart his bowl (for his safety and for your purse!).

CLEANING SUPPLIES

Until a pup is housetrained you will be doing a lot of cleaning. Accidents will occur, which is acceptable in the beginning because the puppy does not know any better. All you can do is be prepared to clean up any 'accidents.' Old rags, towels, newspapers and a safe disinfectant are good to have on hand.

BEYOND THE BASICS

The items previously discussed are the bare necessities. You will find out what else you need as you go along—grooming supplies, flea/tick protection,

CHOOSING THE PROPER COLLAR

The **BUCKLE COLLAR** is the standard collar used for everyday purpose. Be sure that you adjust the buckle on growing puppies. Check it every day. It can become too tight overnight! These collars can be made of leather or nylon. Attach your dog's identification tags to this collar.

The **CHOKE COLLAR** is the usual collar recommended for training. It is constructed of highly polished steel so that it slides easily through the stainless steel loop. The idea is that the dog controls the pressure around its neck and he will stop pulling if the collar becomes uncomfortable. Never leave a choke collar on your dog when not training.

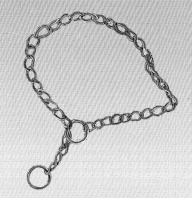

The **HALTER** is for a trained dog that has to be restrained to prevent running away, chasing a cat and the like. Considered the most humane of all collars, it is frequently used on smaller dogs for which collars are not comfortable.

NATURAL TOXINS

Examine your grass and garden landscaping before bringing your puppy home. Many varieties of plants have leaves, stems or flowers that are toxic if ingested, and you can depend on a curious puppy to investigate them. Ask your vet for information on poisonous plants or research them at your library.

baby gates to partition a room, etc. These things will vary depending on your situation but it is important that you have everything you need to feed and make your Belgian Shepherd comfortable in his first few days at home.

PUPPY-PROOFING YOUR HOME

Aside from making sure that your Belgian Shepherd will be comfortable in your home, you also have to make sure that your home is safe for your Belgian Shepherd. This means taking precautions that your pup will

not get into anything he should not get into and that there is nothing within his reach that may harm him should he sniff it, chew it, inspect it, etc. This probably seems obvious since, while you are primarily concerned with your pup's safety, at the same time you do not want your belongings to be ruined. Breakables should be placed out of reach if your dog is to have full run of the house. If he is to be limited to certain places within the house, keep any potentially dangerous items in the 'off-limits' areas. An electrical cord can pose a danger should the puppy decide to taste it—and who is going to convince a pup that it would not make a great chew toy? Cords should be fastened tightly against the wall. If your dog is going to spend time in a crate, make sure that there is nothing near his crate that he can reach if he sticks his curious little nose or paws through the openings. Just as

PUPPY-PROOFING

Thoroughly puppy-proof your house before bringing your puppy home. Never use roach or rodent poisons in any area accessible to the puppy. Avoid the use of toilet cleaners. Most dogs are born with 'toilet sonar' and will take a drink if the lid is left open. Also keep the rubbish secured and out of reach.

CHEMICAL TOXINS

Scour your garage for potential puppy dangers. Remove weed killers, pesticides and antifreeze materials. Antifreeze is highly toxic and even a few drops can kill an adult dog. The sweet taste attracts the animal, who will quickly consume it from the floor or curbside.

you would with a child, keep all household cleaners and chemicals where the pup cannot reach them.

It is also important to make sure that the outside of your home is safe. Of course your puppy should never be unsupervised, but a pup let loose in the garden will want to run and explore, and he should be granted that freedom. Do not let a fence give you a false sense of security; you would be surprised how crafty (and persistent) a dog can be in working out how to dig under and squeeze his way through small holes, or to jump or climb over a fence. The remedy is to make the fence well embedded into the ground and high enough so that it really is impossible for your dog to get over it (about 3 metres should suffice). Be sure to repair or secure any gaps in the fence. Check the fence periodically to ensure that it is in good shape and make repairs as needed; a

very determined pup may return to the same spot to 'work on it' until he is able to get through.

FIRST TRIP TO THE VET

You have selected your puppy, and your home and family are ready. Now all you have to do is collect your Belgian Shepherd from the breeder and the fun begins, right? Well...not so fast. Something else you need to prepare is your pup's first trip to the veterinary surgeon. Perhaps the breeder can recommend someone in the area that knows

A puppy's curiosity will lead him to investigate everything in his world—both indoors and out. Keep a watchful eye on him at all times.

TOXIC PLANTS

Many plants can be toxic to dogs. If you see your dog carrying a piece of vegetation in his mouth, approach him in a quiet, disinterested manner, avoid eye contact, pet him and gradually remove the plant from his mouth. Alternatively, offer him a treat and maybe he'll drop the plant on his own accord. Be sure no toxic plants are growing in your own garden.

Do not overwhelm your new Belgian charge. Let him get accustomed to his new surroundings before introducing him to the entire family, neighbourhood and town.

HOW VACCINES WORK

If you've just bought a puppy, you surely know the importance of having your pup vaccinated, but do you understand how vaccines work? Vaccines contain the same bacteria or viruses that cause the disease you want to prevent, but they have been chemically modified so that they don't cause any harm. Instead, the vaccine causes your dog to produce antibodies that fight the harmful bacteria. Thus, if your pup is exposed to the disease in the future, the antibodies will destroy the viruses or bacteria.

Belgian Shepherds, or maybe you know some other Belgian Shepherd owners who can suggest a good vet. Either way, you should have an appointment arranged for your pup before you pick him up.

The pup's first visit will consist of an overall examination to make sure that the pup does not have any problems that are not apparent to the eye. The veterinary surgeon will also set up a schedule for the pup's vaccinations; the breeder will inform you of which ones the pup has already received and the vet can continue from there.

INTRODUCTION TO THE FAMILY

Everyone in the house will be excited about the puppy coming home and will want to pet him and play with him, but it is best to make the introduction low-key so as not to overwhelm the puppy. He is apprehensive already. It is the first time he has been separated from his mother and the breeder, and the ride to your home is likely to be the first time he has been in a car. The last thing you want to do is smother him, as this will only frighten him further. This is not to say that human contact is not extremely necessary at this stage, because this is the time when a connection between the pup and his human family is formed. Gentle petting and soothing words should help console him, as well as just putting him down and letting him explore on his own (under your watchful eye, of course).

The pup may approach the family members or may busy

TRAVEL TIP

Taking your dog from the breeder to your home in a car can be a very uncomfortable experience for both of you. The puppy will have been taken from his warm, friendly, safe environment and brought into a strange new environment. An environment that moves! Be prepared for loose bowels, urination, crying, whining and even fear biting. With proper love and encouragement when you arrive home, the stress of the trip should quickly disappear.

himself with exploring for a while. Gradually, each person should spend some time with the pup, one at a time, crouching down to get as close to the pup's level as possible and letting him sniff their hands and petting him gently. He definitely needs human attention and he needs to be touched—this is how to form an immediate bond. Just remember that the pup is experiencing a lot of things for the first time, at the same time. There are new people, new noises, new smells, and new things to investigate: so be gentle, be affectionate, and be as comforting as you can be.

PUP'S FIRST NIGHT HOME
You have travelled home with your new charge safely in his crate. He's been to the vet for a thorough check-up; he's been weighed, his papers examined; perhaps he's even been vaccinated and wormed as well. He's met the family, licked the whole family, including the excited children and the less-than-happy cat. He's explored his area, his new bed, the garden and anywhere else he's been permitted. He's eaten his first meal at home and relieved himself in the proper place. He's heard lots of new sounds, smelled new friends and seen more of the outside world than ever before.

That was just the first day! He's worn out and is ready for bed...or so you think!

It's puppy's first night and you are ready to say 'Good night'—keep in mind that this is puppy's first night ever to be sleeping alone. His dam and littermates are no longer at paw's length and he's a bit scared, cold and lonely. Be reassuring to your new family member. This is not the time to spoil him and give in to his inevitable whining.

Puppies whine. They whine to let others know where they are and hopefully to get company out of it. Place your pup in his new bed or crate in his room and close the door. Mercifully, he may fall asleep without a peep. When the inevitable occurs, ignore the whining: he is fine. Be strong and keep his interest in mind. Do not allow yourself to feel guilty and visit the pup. He will fall asleep eventually.

Many breeders recommend placing a piece of bedding from his former home in his new bed so that he recognises the scent of his littermates. Others still advise placing a hot water bottle in his bed for warmth. This latter may be a good idea provided the pup doesn't attempt to suckle—he'll get good and wet and may not fall asleep so fast.

Puppy's first night can be somewhat stressful for the pup and his new family. Remember that you are setting the tone of nighttime at your house. Unless you want to play with your pup every evening at 10 p.m., midnight and 2 a.m., don't initiate the habit. Your family will thank you, and so will your pup!

PREVENTING PUPPY PROBLEMS

SOCIALISATION

Now that you have done all of the preparatory work and have helped your pup get accustomed to his new home and family, it is about time for you to have some fun! Socialising your Belgian Shepherd pup gives you the opportunity to show off your new friend, and your pup gets to reap the benefits of being an adorable furry creature that people will want to pet and, in general, think is absolutely precious!

Besides getting to know his new family, your puppy should be exposed to other people, animals and situations, but of course he must not come into close contact with dogs you don't know well until his course of injections is fully complete. This will help him become well adjusted as he grows up and less prone to being timid or fearful of

the new things he will encounter. Your pup's socialisation began with the breeder but now it is your responsibility to continue it. The socialisation he receives up until the age of 12 weeks is the most critical, as this is the time when he forms his impressions of the outside world. Be especially careful during the socialisation period. The interaction he receives during this time should be gentle and reassuring. Lack of socialisation can manifest itself

MANNERS MATTER

During the   process, a puppy should meet people, experience different environments and definitely be exposed to other canines. Through playing and interacting with other dogs, your puppy will learn lessons, ranging from controlling the pressure of his jaws by biting his litter mates to the inner-workings of the canine pack that he will apply to his human relationships for the rest of his life. That is why removing a puppy from its litter too early (before eight weeks) can be detrimental to the pup's development.

Your Belgian Shepherd puppy is most impressionable, like a dry sponge awaiting moisture. Don't be surprised if he soaks up everything you teach him in no time.

in fear and aggression as the dog grows up. He needs lots of human contact, affection, handling and exposure to other animals.

Once your pup has received his necessary vaccinations, feel free to take him out and about (on his lead, of course). Walk him around the neighbourhood, take him on your daily errands, let people pet him, let him meet other dogs and pets, etc. Puppies do not have to try to make friends; there will be no shortage of people who will want to introduce themselves. Just make sure that you carefully supervise each meeting. If the neighbourhood children want to say hello, for example, that is great—children and pups most often make great companions. Sometimes an excited child can unintentionally handle a pup too roughly, or an overzealous pup can playfully nip a little too

SOCIALISATION

Thorough socialisation includes not only meeting new people but also being introduced to new experiences such as riding in the car, having his coat brushed, hearing the television, walking in a crowd—the list is endless. The more your pup experiences, and the more positive the experiences are, the less of a shock and the less frightening it will be for your pup to encounter new things.

hard. You want to make socialisation experiences positive ones. What a pup learns during this very formative stage will affect his attitude toward future encounters. You want your dog to be comfortable around everyone. A pup that has a bad experience with a child may grow up to be a dog that is shy around or aggressive toward children.

CONSISTENCY IN TRAINING

Dogs, being pack animals, naturally need a leader, or else they try to establish dominance in their packs. When you welcome a dog into your family, the choice of who becomes the leader and who becomes the 'pack' is entirely up to you! Your pup's intuitive quest for dominance, coupled with the fact that it is nearly impossible to look at an adorable Belgian Shepherd pup with his 'puppy-dog' eyes and not cave in, give the pup almost an unfair advantage in getting the upper hand! A pup will definitely test the waters to see what he can and cannot do. Do not give in to those pleading eyes—stand your ground when it comes to disciplining the pup and make sure that all family members do the same. It will only confuse the pup when Mother tells him to get off the sofa when he is used to sitting up there with

PROPER SOCIALISATION
The socialisation period for puppies is from age 8 to 16 weeks. This is the time when puppies need to leave their birth family and take up residence with their new owners, where they will meet many new people, other pets, etc. Failure to be adequately socialised can cause the dog to grow up fearing others and being shy and unfriendly due to a lack of self-confidence.

Father to watch the nightly news. Avoid discrepancies by having all members of the household decide on the rules before the pup even comes home...and be consistent in enforcing them! Early training shapes the dog's personality, so you cannot be unclear in what you expect.

NO CHOCOLATE!

Use treats to bribe your dog into a desired behaviour. Try small pieces of hard cheese or freeze-dried liver. Never offer chocolate as it has toxic qualities for dogs.

COMMON PUPPY PROBLEMS

The best way to prevent puppy problems is to be proactive in stopping an undesirable behaviour as soon as it starts. The old saying 'You can't teach an old dog new tricks' does not necessarily hold true, but it is true that it is much easier to discourage bad behaviour in a young developing pup than to wait until the pup's bad behaviour becomes the adult dog's bad habit. There are some problems that are especially prevalent in puppies as they develop.

NIPPING

As puppies start to teethe, they feel the need to sink their teeth into anything available...unfortunately that includes your fingers, arms, hair and toes. You may find this behaviour cute for the first five seconds...until you feel just how sharp those puppy teeth are. This is something you want to discourage immediately and consistently with a firm 'No!' (or whatever number of firm 'No's' it takes for him to understand that you mean business). Then replace your finger with an appropriate chew toy. While this behaviour is merely annoying when the dog is young, it can become dangerous as your Belgian Shepherd's adult teeth grow in and his jaws develop, and he continues to think it is okay to gnaw on human appendages. Your Belgian Shepherd does not mean any harm with a friendly nip, but he also does not know his own strength.

CRYING/WHINING

Your pup will often cry, whine, whimper, howl or make some type of commotion when he is left alone. This is basically his way of calling out for attention to make sure that you know he is there and that you have not forgotten about him. He feels insecure when he is left alone, when you are out of the house and he is in his crate or when you are in another part of the house and he cannot see you. The noise he is making is an expression of the anxiety he feels at being alone, so he needs to be taught that being alone is okay. You are not actually training the dog to stop making noise, you are training him to feel comfortable when he is alone and thus removing the need for him to make the noise. This is where the crate with cosy bedding and a toy comes in handy. You want to know that he is safe when you are not there to supervise, and you know that he will be safe in his crate rather than roaming freely about the house. In order for the pup to stay in his crate without making a fuss, he needs to be comfort-able in his crate. On that note, it is extremely important that the crate is never used as a form of punishment, or the pup will have a negative association with the crate.

Accustom the pup to the crate in short, gradually increasing time intervals in which you put him in the crate, maybe with a treat, and stay in the room with him. If he cries or makes a fuss, do not go to him, but stay in his sight. Gradually he will realise that staying in his crate is all right without your help, and it will not be so traumatic for him when you are not around. You may want to leave the radio on softly when you leave the house; the sound of human voices may be comforting to him.

CHEWING TIPS

Chewing goes hand in hand with nipping in the sense that a teething puppy is always looking for a way to soothe his aching gums. In this case, instead of chewing on you, he may have taken a liking to your favourite shoe or something else which he should not be chewing. Again, realise that this is a normal canine behaviour that does not need to be discouraged, only redirected. Your pup just needs to be taught what is acceptable to chew on and what is off limits. Consistently tell him NO when you catch him chewing on something forbidden and give him a chew toy. Conversely, praise him when you catch him chewing on something appropriate. In this way you are discouraging the inappropriate behaviour and reinforcing the desired behaviour. The puppy chewing should stop after his adult teeth have come in, but an adult dog continues to chew for various reasons—perhaps because he is bored, perhaps to relieve tension or perhaps he just likes to chew. That is why it is important to redirect his chewing when he is still young.

DIETARY AND FEEDING CONSIDERATIONS

Today the choices of food for your Belgian Shepherd are many and varied. There are simply dozens of brands of food in all sorts of flavours and textures, ranging from puppy diets to those for seniors. There are even hypoallergenic and low-calorie diets available. Because your Belgian Shepherd's food has a bearing on coat, health and temperament, it is essential that the most suitable diet is selected for a Belgian Shepherd of his age. It is fair to say, however, that even experienced owners can be perplexed by the enormous range of foods available. Only understanding what is best for your dog will help you reach a valued decision.

Dog foods are produced in three basic types: dried, semi-moist and tinned. Dried foods are useful for the cost-conscious for overall they tend to be less expensive than semi-moist or tinned. They also contain the least fat and the most preservatives. In general, tinned foods are made up of 60–70 percent water, while semi-moist ones often contain so much sugar that they are perhaps the least preferred by owners, even though their dogs seem to like them.

When selecting your dog's diet, three stages of development must be considered: the puppy stage, adult stage and the senior or veteran stage.

Puppy Stage

Puppies instinctively want to suck milk from their mother's teats and a normal puppy will exhibit this behaviour from just a few moments following birth. If

FEEDING TIP
You must store your dried dog food carefully. Open packages of dog food quickly lose their vitamin value, usually within 90 days of being opened. Mould spores and vermin could also contaminate the food.

puppies do not attempt to suckle within the first half-hour or so, they should be encouraged to do so by placing them on the nipples, having selected ones with plenty of milk. This early milk supply is important in providing colostrum to protect the puppies during the first eight to ten weeks of their lives. Although a mother's milk is much better than any milk formula, despite there being some excellent ones available, if the puppies do not feed, you will have to feed them yourself. For

TEST FOR PROPER DIET

A good test for proper diet is the colour, odour and firmness of your dog's stool. A healthy dog usually produces three semi-hard stools per day. The stools should have no unpleasant odour. They should be the same colour from excretion to excretion.

those with less experience, advice from a veterinary surgeon is important so that you feed not only the right quantity of milk but that of correct quality, fed at suitably frequent intervals, usually every two hours during the first few days of life.

Puppies should be allowed to nurse from their mothers for about the first six weeks, although from the third or fourth week you should begin to introduce small portions of suitable solid food.

GRAIN-BASED DIETS

Some less expensive dog foods are based on grains and other plant proteins. While these products may appear to be attractively priced, many breeders prefer a diet based on animal proteins and believe that they are more conducive to your dog's health. Many grain-based diets rely on soy protein that may cause flatulence (passing gas).

There are many cases, however, when your dog might require a special diet. These special requirements should only be recommended by your veterinary surgeon.

Most breeders like to introduce alternate milk and meat meals initially, building up to weaning time.

By the time the puppies are seven or a maximum of eight weeks old, they should be fully weaned and fed solely on a

Competition for dinner sharpens the puppies' appetites. Once your Belgian pup comes home, he may not eat with the same gusto, but his appetite will return once he's comfortable in your home.

months of age. Again you should rely upon your veterinary surgeon or dietary specialist to recommend an acceptable maintenance diet. Major dog food manufacturers specialise in this type of food, and it is merely necessary for you to select the one best suited to your dog's needs. Active dogs may have different requirements than sedate dogs.

SENIOR DIETS

As dogs get older, their metabolism changes. The older dog usually exercises less, moves

There is simply no better food for the young puppy under six weeks of age than its mother's milk.

proprietary puppy food. Selection of the most suitable, good-quality diet at this time is essential, for a puppy's fastest growth rate is during the first year of life. Veterinary surgeons are usually able to offer advice in this regard and, although the frequency of meals will have been reduced over time, only when a young dog has reached the age of about 12 months should an adult diet be fed.

Puppy and junior diets should be well balanced for the needs of your dog, so that except in certain circumstances additional vitamins, minerals and proteins will not be required.

ADULT DIETS

A dog is considered an adult when it has stopped growing, so in general the diet of a Belgian Shepherd can be changed to an adult one at about 10 to 12

FEEDING TIP

Dog food must be at room temperature, neither too hot nor too cold. Fresh water, changed daily and served in a clean bowl, is mandatory, especially when feeding dried food.

Never feed your dog from the table while you are eating. Never feed your dog leftovers from your own meal. They usually contain too much fat and too much seasoning.

Dogs must chew their food. Hard pellets are excellent; soups and slurries are to be avoided.

Don't add left-overs or any extras to normal dog food. The normal food is usually balanced and adding something extra destroys the balance.

Except for age-related changes, dogs do not require dietary variations. They can be fed the same diet, day after day, without their becoming ill.

more slowly and sleeps more. This change in lifestyle and physiological performance requires a change in diet. Since these changes take place slowly, they might not be recognisable. What is easily recognisable is weight gain. By continuing to feed

your dog an adult-maintenance diet when it is slowing down metabolically, your dog will gain weight. Obesity in an older dog compounds the health problems that already accompany old age.

As your dog gets older, few of his organs function up to par. The kidneys slow down and the intestines become less efficient. These age-related factors are best

FOOD PREFERENCE

Selecting the best dried dog food is difficult. There is no majority consensus among veterinary scientists as to the value of nutrient analyses (protein, fat, fibre, moisture, ash, cholesterol, minerals, etc.). All agree that feeding trials are what matters, but you also have to consider the individual dog. Its weight, age, activity and what pleases its taste, all must be considered. It is probably best to take the advice of your veterinary surgeon. Every dog's dietary requirements vary, even during the lifetime of a particular dog.

If your dog is fed a good dried food, it does not require supplements of meat or vegetables. Dogs do appreciate a little variety in their diets so you may choose to stay with the same brand, but vary the flavour. Alternatively you may wish to add a little flavoured stock to give a difference to the taste.

Senior Belgian Shepherds will not require the same amount of food as an active adult. Adjust your senior's diet accordingly.

DO DOGS HAVE TASTE BUDS?

Watching a dog 'wolf' or gobble his food, seemingly without chewing, leads an owner to wonder whether their dogs can taste anything. Yes, dogs have taste buds, with sensory perception of sweet, salty and sour. Puppies are born with fully mature taste buds.

handled with a change in diet and a change in feeding schedule to give smaller portions that are more easily digested.

There is no single best diet for every older dog. While many dogs do well on light or senior diets, other dogs do better on puppy diets or other special premium diets such as lamb and rice. Be sensitive to your senior Belgian Shepherd's diet and this will help

What are you feeding your dog.

Read the label on your dog food. Many dog foods only advise what 50–55% of the contents are, leaving the other 45% in doubt.

- 1.3% Calcium
- 1.6% Fatty Acids
- 4.6% Crude Fibre
- 11% Moisture
- 14% Crude Fat
- 22% Crude Protein
- **45.5% ? ? ?**

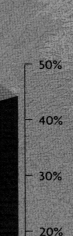

50%

40%

30%

20%

10%

0%

control other problems that may arise with your old friend.

WATER

Just as your dog needs proper nutrition from his food, water is an essential 'nutrient' as well. Water keeps the dog's body properly hydrated and promotes normal function of the body's systems. During housebreaking it is necessary to keep an eye on how much water your Belgian Shepherd is drinking, but once he is reliably trained he should have access to clean fresh water at all times, especially if you feed dried food. Make certain that the dog's water bowl is clean, and change the water often.

TIPPING THE SCALES

Good nutrition is vital to your dog's health, but many people end up over-feeding or giving unnecessary supplements. Here are some common doggie diet don'ts:

• Adding milk, yoghurt and cheese to your dog's diet may seem like a good idea for coat and skin care, but dairy products are very fattening and can cause indigestion.

• Diets high in fat will not cause heart attacks in dogs but will certainly cause your dog to gain weight.

• Most importantly, don't assume your dog will simply stop eating once he doesn't need any more food. Given the chance, he will eat you out of house and home!

DRINK, DRANK, DRUNK— MAKE IT A DOUBLE

In both humans and dogs, as well as most living organisms, water forms the major part of nearly every body tissue. Naturally, we take water for granted, but without it, life as we know it would cease.

For dogs, water is needed to keep their bodies functioning biochemically. Additionally, water is needed to replace the water lost while panting. Unlike humans who are able to sweat to dissipate heat, dogs must pant to cool down, thereby losing the vital water from their bodies needed to regulate their body temperatures. Humans lose electrolyte-containing products and other body-fluid components through sweating; dogs do not lose anything except water.

Water is essential always, but especially so when the weather is hot or humid or when your dog is exercising or working vigorously.

EXERCISE

The Belgian Shepherd thrives on physical stimulation and activity. Owners who cannot offer their dogs abundant exercise will not enjoy the company of happy Belgian Shepherds. A sedentary lifestyle is very harmful to this breed and the dog can adopt many unacceptable behaviours if he is not properly exercised.

Few breeds are as talented as the Belgian Shepherd, and its physical abilities are boundless. Your Belgian Shepherd will welcome daily walks on a loose lead or a flexible lead. Free running is the best type of exercise for your dog, but never allow your Belgian Shepherd off lead unless you are in an enclosed field or some other safe area. The beach or an open field is an ideal location for the Belgian Shepherd to release his pent-up energy and spirit. Since the breed was designed to run and work vigorously from sunrise to sunset, it is no mystery why this majestic athlete needs a couple of hours of invigorating activity to keep fit physically and mentally. Remember a well-exercised Belgian Shepherd is a happy one, and a happy dog is so much easier to train, live with and love.

GROOMING

MAINTAINING THE COAT

Grooming the coat should be a pleasant task, not only to make your dog look more beautiful but also to keep the coat and skin healthy. Begin grooming when your Belgian Shepherd is a puppy using a bench or a table. Adult dogs seem to prefer the stability of the floor and they can be groomed while lying on their blanket. By removing dead hair and dust, you keep your dog's coat glossy and his appearance neat. Regular grooming also eliminates the necessity of bathing.

Daily grooming of the coat is well advised. It stimulates the blood circulation and guarantees a good coat condition. Brushing is beneficial for the dog's character, as he bonds with his groomer and learns to submit to the authority of his master; it is part of standard obedience. While grooming is comforting to most dogs, some

> ## EXERCISE ALERT!
> You should be careful where you exercise your dog. Many country-side areas have been sprayed with chemicals that are highly toxic to both dogs and humans. Never allow your dog to eat grass or drink from puddles on either public or private grounds, as the run-off water may contain chemicals from sprays and herbicides.

dominant dogs may resent it, so you should introduce grooming routines as soon as you acquire your new pup.

The grooming of a Malinois, the short-haired Belgian Shepherd, is very simple and easy. He can be groomed weekly, but during moults preferably every two days. A simple combing or brushing and smoothing out of the coat are sufficient. A metal comb with a handle can be used to remove loose hairs and to

Few breeds are as naturally athletic as the Belgian Shepherd. This Malinois effortlessly flies over the jump at a working trial.

untangle any mats or knots. Be careful to avoid damaging or irritating the skin. The hairs may not be broken or pulled out. For this reason the teeth of the comb should be well spaced with smooth and rounded points. Instead of a comb, a slicker or a bristle brush can also be used to remove dead hair from the coat. After combing or brushing, you can go over the dog with a rubber fingered grooming device or a wire grooming glove.

Although the kind of equipment you will need depends on the coat length and texture, basically the same tools used for the Malinois can be used for the long-haired varieties, the Groenendael and the Tervueren. For long coats, however, grooming is more time-consuming and daily care is required, especially during the moulting seasons. A slicker brush is the best grooming tool to eliminate loose coat and to separate the hairs. A large-size slicker brush should be used, with fine, short wire teeth, set close together in a rubber base. A firm bristle brush, with nylon and/or natural bristles, set in a cushioned base with a handle, can also be used. A boar-bristle brush is often preferred for show-grooming because it is gentler and prevents damaging the skin and coat. The comb can be used not only for the feathers around the ears, on the legs and on the tail but also as a finishing tool to put final touches on the coat. Use a comb with medium-spaced teeth. When the teeth of the comb are too closely set, it does not pass through the coat easily; and when they are spaced too far apart, it fails to remove loose hairs. Blunt-ended scissors (surgical type) can be used to trim any hair that has grown long between the toes.

For your long-haired Belgian Shepherd, the routine grooming should be established as a basic ritual, always using the same technique. Your dog can be groomed when standing, but when he is strong-willed you should command him to lie down on his side. In this position, it is easier to reach parts of the body, such as the stomach and the insides of the legs. Begin by holding a section of hair open with your hand and then, following the lay of the coat, you brush or comb the section below your hand. You continue this way until you have groomed the entire coat. You can use a softer brush on the belly and flanks. Make your dog stand to groom the back, neck, chest, legs and feet. Thoroughly brush or comb through the feathery hair behind the ears, the rear side of the legs, the tail and the inside of the thighs to remove tangles or stray strands of hair. It is possible to work out tangles of hair with the fingers, always being careful not

All dogs, regardless of their type of coat, require brushing and grooming of one sort or another. Start the brush training while the puppy is young.

Your local pet shop will have a variety of grooming tools with which you can keep your Belgian Shepherd's coat in peak condition.

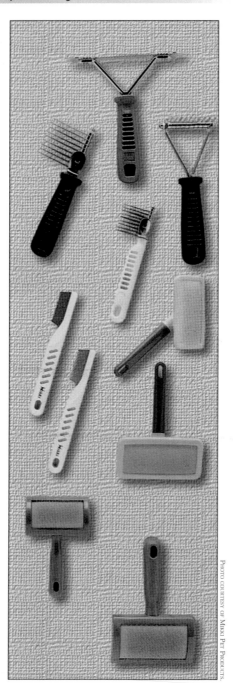

PHOTO COURTESY OF MIKKI PET PRODUCTS.

to hurt the dog. Flattening the coat on the body completes the grooming; use the comb or a glove made for this purpose.

Grooming your long-haired Belgian Shepherd for the show ring is not really different from basic grooming for the home. If you intend to show your dog, you must understand what the breed standard calls for. The Belgian Shepherd's type depends on his general outline or silhouette. For a long-haired Belgian Shepherd especially, the coat needs to be 'shaped' in accordance with the description set forth in the standard. By proper show grooming, which supposes thorough breed knowledge, a silhouette can be made to appear more character-

GROOMING EQUIPMENT

How much grooming equipment you purchase will depend on how much grooming you are going to do. Here are some basics:

- Natural bristle brush
- Slicker brush
- Metal comb
- Scissors
- Blaster
- Rubber mat
- Dog shampoo
- Spray hose attachment
- Ear cleaner
- Cotton wipes
- Towels
- Nail clippers

istic or more typical.

The Laekenois or rough-haired Belgian Shepherd is the most difficult to groom. The process is called 'plucking' and 'trimming.' It is done by removing excess hair by hand and by using a stripping knife. It can take several hours to trim a Laekenois and needs to be done by a real expert. As a result, the final silhouette of the Laekenois is more attractive and neat than in the natural state.

BATHING

You should not bath your Belgian Shepherd more frequently than necessary. It is rare that a dog who has been properly and regularly brushed will need frequent bathing. You should only bath

SOAP IT UP

The use of human soap products like shampoo, bubble bath and hand soap can be damaging to a dog's coat and skin. Human products are too strong and remove the protective oils coating the dog's hair and skin (making him water-resistant). Use only shampoo made especially for dogs and you may like to use a medicated shampoo, which will always help to keep external parasites at bay.

BATHING BEAUTY

Once you are sure that the dog is thoroughly rinsed, squeeze the excess water out of the coat with your hand and dry him with a heavy towel. You may choose to use a blaster on his coat or just let it dry naturally. In cold weather, never allow your dog outside with a wet coat.

There are 'dry bath' products on the market, which are sprays and powders intended for spot cleaning, that can be used between regular baths, if necessary. They are not substitutes for regular baths, but they are easy to use for touch-ups as they do not require rinsing.

your Belgian Shepherd when he has become soiled with dirt or foreign substances not easily removed by brushing. Remember that soap removes the natural oil from the hair and skin. A good dog soap (not human brand shampoo) and thorough rinsing are recommended.

If you accustom your pup to being bathed as a puppy, it will be second nature by the time he grows up. You want your dog to be at ease in the bath or else it could end up a wet, soapy, messy ordeal for both of you!

Brush your Belgian Shepherd thoroughly before wetting his coat. This will get rid of most mats and tangles, which are harder to remove when the coat is wet. Make certain that your dog has a good non-slip surface to stand on. Begin by wetting the dog's coat. A shower or hose attachment is necessary for thoroughly wetting and rinsing the coat. Check the water temperature to make sure that it is neither too hot nor too cold.

Next, apply dog soap to the coat and work it into a good lather. Wash the head last; you do not want shampoo to drip into the dog's eyes while you are washing the rest of his body. Work the shampoo all the way down to the skin. You can use this opportunity to check the skin for any bumps, bites or other abnormalities. Do not neglect any area of the body—get all of the hard-to-reach places.

Once the dog has been

Cleaning your dog's ears is a part of grooming. Get instructions from your veterinary surgeon regarding how to clean and inspect your dog's ears.

thoroughly shampooed, he requires an equally thorough rinsing. Shampoo left in the coat can be irritating to the skin. Protect his eyes from the shampoo by shielding them with your hand and directing the flow of water in the opposite direction. You should also avoid getting water in the ear canal. Be prepared for your dog to shake out his coat—you might want to stand back, but make sure you have a hold on the dog to keep him from running through the house.

EAR CLEANING

The ears should be kept clean with a cotton wipe and ear powder made especially for dogs. Be on the lookout for any signs of infection or ear mite infestation. If your Belgian Shepherd has been shaking his head or scratching at his ears frequently, this usually indicates a problem. If his ears have an unusual odour, this is a sure sign of mite infestation or infection, and a signal to have his ears checked by the veterinary surgeon.

NAIL CLIPPING

Your Belgian Shepherd should be accustomed to having his nails trimmed at an early age, since it will be part of your maintenance routine throughout his life. Not only does it look nicer, but long nails can scratch someone unintentionally. Also, a long nail

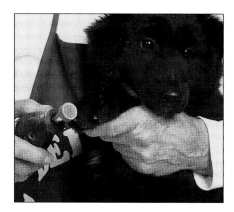

Nail Maintenance

Nail Casing

Quick

Cut Line

Dark-Coloured Nails

With black or dark nails, where the quick is not easy to see, it's best to clip only the tip of the nail or to use a file.

Light-Coloured Nails

In light-coloured nails, clipping is much simpler because you can see the vein (or quick) that grows inside the casing.

Clipping or grinding down your Belgian Shepherd's nails is a must unless the dog spends a lot of time walking on hard surfaces.

Clip only the bottom portion of the nail, avoiding the quick. If you cut into the quick, the nail will bleed and the dog will experience pain. A styptic pencil will stop the bleeding. Reassure the injured dog by talking quietly to him.

has a better chance of ripping and bleeding, or causing the feet to spread. A good rule of thumb is that if you can hear your dog's nails clicking on the floor when he walks, his nails are too long.

Before you start cutting, make sure you can identify the 'quick' in each nail. The quick is a blood vessel that runs through the centre of each nail and grows rather close to the end. It will bleed if accidentally cut, which will be quite painful for the dog as it contains nerve endings. Keep some type of clotting agent on hand, such as a styptic pencil or styptic powder (the type used for shaving). This will stop the bleeding quickly when applied to the end of the cut nail. Do not panic if you cut the quick, just stop the bleeding and talk soothingly to your dog. Once he has calmed down, move on to the next nail. It is better to clip a little at a time, particularly with black-nailed dogs.

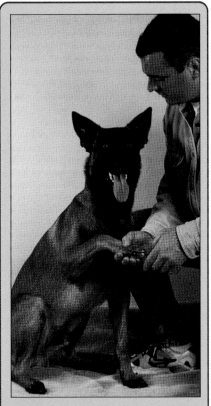

PEDICURE TIP

A dog that spends a lot of time outside on a hard surface, such as cement or pavement, will have his nails naturally worn down and may not need to have them trimmed as often, except maybe in the colder months when he is not outside as much. Regardless, it is best to get your dog accustomed to this procedure at an early age so that he is used to it. Some dogs are especially sensitive about having their feet touched, but if a dog has experienced it since he was young, he should not be bothered by it.

Hold your pup steady as you begin trimming his nails; you do not want him to make any sudden movements or run away. Talk to him soothingly and stroke him as you clip. Holding his foot in your hand, simply take off the end of each nail in one quick clip. You can purchase nail clippers that are specially made for dogs; you can probably find them wherever you buy pet or grooming supplies.

TRAVELLING WITH YOUR DOG

CAR TRAVEL

You should accustom your Belgian Shepherd to riding in a car at an early age. You may or may not take him in the car often, but at the very least he will need to go to the vet and you do not want these trips to be traumatic for the dog or troublesome for you. The safest way for a dog to ride in the car is in his crate. If he uses a crate in the house, you can use the same crate for travel.

Put the pup in the crate and see how he reacts. If he seems uneasy, you can have a passenger hold him on his lap while you drive. Another option is a specially made safety harness for dogs, which straps the dog in much like a seat belt. Do not let the dog roam loose in the vehicle—this is very dangerous! If you should stop short, your dog can be thrown and injured. If the dog starts climbing on you and pestering you while you are driving, you will not be able to concentrate on the road. It is an unsafe situation for everyone—human and canine.

For long trips, be prepared to stop to let the dog relieve himself. Take with you whatever you need to clean up after him, including some paper kitchen towels and perhaps some old towelling for use should he have an accident in the car or suffer from travel sickness.

AIR TRAVEL

While it is possible to take a dog on a flight within Britain, this is fairly unusual and advance permission is always required. The dog will be required to travel in a fibreglass crate and you should always check in advance with the airline regarding specific requirements. To help the dog be at ease, put one of his favourite toys in the crate with him. Do not feed the dog for at least six hours before the trip to minimise his need to relieve himself. However,

TRAVEL TIP
Never leave your dog alone in the car. In hot weather your dog can die from the high temperature inside a closed vehicle; even a car parked in the shade can heat up very quickly. Leaving the window open is dangerous as well since the dog can hurt himself trying to get out.

certain regulations specify that water must always be made available to the dog in the crate.

Make sure your dog is properly identified and that your contact information appears on his ID tags and on his crate. Animals travel in a different area

Show dogs travel more than any other dogs. If your Belgian Shepherd will pursue a career as a show dog, it is wise to acclimate him to the crate and the car immediately.

ON THE ROAD
If you are going on a long motor trip with your dog, be sure the hotels are dog friendly. Many hotels do not accept dogs. Also take along some ice that can be thawed and offered to your dog if he becomes overheated. Most dogs like to lick ice.

95

Belgian Shepherds need considerable exercise on a daily basis. If he's deprived of the chance to stretch his limbs, he can become bored and destructive.

TRAVEL TIP
When travelling, never let your dog off-lead in a strange area. Your dog could run away out of fear or decide to chase a passing squirrel or cat or simply want to stretch his legs without restriction—you might never see your canine friend again.

of the plane than human passengers so every rule must be strictly adhered to so as to prevent the risk of getting separated from your dog.

BOARDING

So you want to take a family holiday—and you want to include all members of the family. You would probably make arrangements for accommodation ahead of time anyway, but this is especially important when travelling with a dog. You do not want to make an overnight stop at the only place around for miles and find out that they do not allow dogs. Also, you do not want to reserve a place for your family without confirming that you are travelling with a dog because if it is against their policy you may not have a place to stay.

Alternatively, if you are travelling and choose not to bring your

You should locate a suitable kennel close to your home, one that is large enough to afford your dog sufficient daily exercise.

Belgian Shepherd, you will have to make arrangements for him while you are away. Some options are to take him to a neighbour's house to stay while you are gone, to have a trusted neighbour pop in often or stay at your house, or bring your dog to a reputable boarding kennel. If you choose to board him at a kennel, you should visit in advance to see the facilities provided, how clean they are

LOST AND FOUND
You have a valuable dog. If the dog is lost or stolen, you would undoubtedly become extremely upset. If you encounter a lost dog, notify the police or the local animal shelter.

and where the dogs are kept. Talk to some of the employees and see how they treat the dogs—do they spend time with the dogs, play with them, exercise them, etc.? Also find out the kennel's policy on vaccinations and what they require. This is for all of the dogs' safety, since when dogs are kept together, there is a greater risk of diseases being passed from dog to dog.

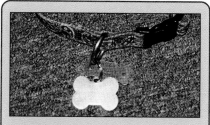

IDENTIFICATION

If your dog gets lost, he is not able to ask for directions home.

Identification tags fastened to the collar give important information—the dog's name, the owner's name, the owner's address and a telephone number where the owner can be reached. This makes it easy for whomever finds the dog to contact the owner and arrange to have the dog returned. An added advantage is that a person will be more likely to approach a lost dog who has ID tags on his collar; it tells the person that this is somebody's pet rather than a stray. This is the easiest and fastest method of identification provided that the tags stay on the collar and the collar stays on the dog.

IDENTIFICATION

Your Belgian Shepherd is your valued companion and friend. That is why you always keep a close eye on him and you have made sure that he cannot escape from the garden or wriggle out of his collar and run away from you. However, accidents can happen and there may come a time when your dog unexpectedly gets separated from you. If this unfortunate event should occur, the first thing on your mind will be finding him. Proper identification, including an ID tag, a tattoo and possibly a microchip, will increase the chances of his being returned to you safely and quickly.

Living with an untrained dog is a lot like owning a piano that you do not know how to play—it is a nice object to look at but it does not do much more than that to bring you pleasure. Now try

TAKING CARE

Science is showing that as people take care of their pets, the pets are taking care of their owners. A study in 1998 published in the *American Journal of Cardiology* found that having a pet can prolong his owner's life. Pet owners have lower blood pressure, and pets help their owners to relax and keep them more physically fit. It was also found that pets help to keep the elderly connected to their community.

taking piano lessons and suddenly the piano comes alive and brings forth magical sounds and rhythms that set your heart singing and your body swaying.

The same is true with your Belgian Shepherd. Any dog is a big responsibility and if not trained sensibly may develop unacceptable behaviour that annoys you or could even cause family friction.

To train your Belgian Shepherd, you may like to enrol in an obedience class. Teach him good manners as you learn how and why he behaves the way he does. Find out how to communicate with your dog and how to recognise and understand his communications with you. Suddenly the dog takes on a new role in your life—he is clever, interesting, well-behaved and fun to be with. He demonstrates his bond of devotion to you daily. In other words, your Belgian Shepherd does wonders for your ego because he constantly reminds you that you are not only his leader, you are his hero!

Those involved with teaching

dog obedience and counselling owners about their dogs' behaviour have discovered some interesting facts about dog ownership. For example, training dogs when they are puppies results in the highest rate of success in developing well-mannered and well-adjusted adult dogs. Training an older dog, from six months to six years of age, can produce almost equal results providing that the owner accepts the dog's slower rate of learning capability and is willing to work patiently to help the dog succeed at developing to his fullest potential. Unfortunately, many owners of untrained adult dogs lack the patience factor, so they

REAP THE REWARDS

If you start with a normal, healthy dog and give him time, patience and some carefully executed lessons, you will reap the rewards of that training for the life of the dog. And what a life it will be! The two of you will find immeasurable pleasure in the companionship you have built together with love, respect and understanding.

do not persist until their dogs are successful at learning particular behaviours.

Training a puppy aged 10 to 16 weeks (20 weeks at the most) is like working with a dry sponge in a pool of water. The pup soaks up whatever you show him and constantly looks for more things to do and learn. At this early age, his body is not yet producing hormones, and therein lies the reason for such a high rate of success. Without hormones, he is focused on his owners and not particularly interested in investigating other places, dogs, people, etc. You are his leader: his provider of food, water, shelter and security. He latches onto you and wants to stay close. He will usually follow you from room to room, will not let you out of his sight when you are outdoors with him and will respond in like manner to the people and animals you encounter. If you greet a

The rewards of a healthy, well-trained Belgian Shepherd are ineffable.

curiosity emerges and he begins to investigate the world around him. It is at this time when you may notice that the untrained dog begins to wander away from you and even ignore your commands to stay close. When this behaviour becomes a problem, the owner has two choices: get rid of the dog or train him. It is strongly urged that you choose the latter option.

There are usually classes within a reasonable distance from the owner's home, but you can also do a lot to train your dog yourself. Sometimes there are classes available but the tuition is too costly. Whatever the circumstances, the solution to the problem of lack of lesson availability lies within the pages of this book.

This chapter is devoted to helping you train your Belgian Shepherd at home. If the recommended procedures are followed faithfully, you may expect positive results that will

friend warmly, he will be happy to greet the person as well. If, however, you are hesitant, even anxious, about the approach of a stranger, he will respond accordingly.

Once the puppy begins to produce hormones, his natural

prove rewarding both to you and your dog.

Whether your new charge is a puppy or a mature adult, the methods of teaching and the techniques we use in training basic behaviours are the same. After all, no dog, whether puppy or adult, likes harsh or inhumane methods. All creatures, however, respond favourably to gentle motivational methods and sincere praise and encouragement. Now let us get started.

HOUSEBREAKING

You can train a puppy to relieve itself wherever you choose, but this must be somewhere suitable. You should bear in mind from the outset that when your puppy is old enough to go out in public places, any canine deposits must be removed at once. You will always have to carry with you a small plastic bag or 'poop-scoop.'

Outdoor training includes

THE HAND THAT FEEDS

To a dog's way of thinking, your hands are like his mouth in terms of a defence mechanism. If you squeeze him too tightly, he might just bite you because that would be his normal response. This is not aggressive biting and, although all biting should be discouraged, you need the discipline in learning how to handle your dog.

such surfaces as grass, soil and cement. Indoor training usually means training your dog to newspaper.

When deciding on the surface and location that you will want your Belgian Shepherd to use, be sure it is going to be permanent. Training your dog to grass and then changing your mind two months later is extremely difficult for both dog and owner.

Next, choose the command you will use each and every time you want your puppy to void. 'Hurry up' and 'Be quick' are examples of commands commonly used by dog owners.

Get in the habit of giving the puppy your chosen relief command before you take him out. That way, when he becomes an adult, you will be able to determine if he wants to go out when you ask him. A confirmation will be signs of interest, wagging his tail, watching you intently, going to the door, etc.

Finding the time to train your dog is tantamount to spending quality time with an animal that thinks the world of you.

SEPARATION ANXIETY

Recognised by behaviourists as the most common form of stress for dogs, separation anxiety can also lead to destructive behaviours in your dog. It's more than your Belgian Shepherd howling his displeasure at your leaving the house and his being left alone. This is a normal reaction, no different from the child who cries as his mother leaves him on the first day at school. In fact, if you are constantly with your dog, he will come to expect you with him all of the time, making it even more traumatic for him when you are not there. Obviously, you enjoy spending time with your dog, and he thrives on your love and attention. However, it should not become a dependent relationship in which he is heartbroken wihout you. This broken heart can also bring on destructive behaviour as well as loss of appetite, depression and lack of interest in play and interaction. With the Belgian Shepherd, boredom and inactivity are tantamount to torture! If you are leaving your Belgian Shepherd home all day with no stimulation beyond a nylon bone in

his crate, he is likely to pine and pout for hours, moping in unhappiness until you arrive. For a dog as intelligent and active as this phenomenal herding dog, this is a daily prison sentence. Canine behaviourists have been expending much energy in helping owners better understand the importance of this stressful condition.

PUPPY'S NEEDS

Puppy needs to relieve himself after play periods, after each meal, after he has been sleeping and at any time he indicates that he is looking for a place to urinate or defecate.

The urinary and intestinal tract muscles of very young puppies are not fully developed. Therefore, like human babies, puppies need to relieve

CANINE DEVELOPMENT SCHEDULE

It is important to understand how and at what age a puppy develops into adulthood. If you are a puppy owner, consult the following Canine Development Schedule to determine the stage of development your puppy is currently experiencing. This knowledge will help you as you work with the puppy in the weeks and months ahead.

Period	Age	Characteristics
FIRST TO THIRD	BIRTH TO SEVEN WEEKS	Puppy needs food, sleep and warmth, and responds to simple and gentle touching. Needs mother for security and disciplining. Needs littermates for learning and interacting with other dogs. Pup learns to function within a pack and learns pack order of dominance. Begin socialising with adults and children for short periods. Begins to become aware of its environment.
FOURTH	EIGHT TO TWELVE WEEKS	Brain is fully developed. Needs socialising with outside world. Remove from mother and littermates. Needs to change from canine pack to human pack. Human dominance necessary. Fear period occurs between 8 and 16 weeks. Avoid fright and pain.
FIFTH	THIRTEEN TO SIXTEEN WEEKS	Training and formal obedience should begin. Less association with other dogs, more with people, places, situations. Period will pass easily if you remember this is pup's change-to-adolescence time. Be firm and fair. Flight instinct prominent. Permissiveness and over-disciplining can do permanent damage. Praise for good behaviour.
JUVENILE	FOUR TO EIGHT MONTHS	Another fear period about 7 to 8 months of age. It passes quickly, but be cautious of fright and pain. Sexual maturity reached. Dominant traits established. Dog should understand sit, down, come and stay by now.

NOTE: THESE ARE APPROXIMATE TIME FRAMES. ALLOW FOR INDIVIDUAL DIFFERENCES IN PUPPIES.

Belgian Shepherd Dog

If there are children in your home, they should be trained to provide the puppy with exercise, toilet relief and compassionate care.

themselves frequently.

Take your puppy out often—every hour for an eight-week-old, for example, and always immediately after sleeping and eating. The older the puppy, the less often he will need to relieve himself. Finally, as a mature healthy adult, he will require only three to five relief trips per day.

HOUSING

Since the types of housing and control you provide for your puppy have a direct relationship on the success of housetraining, we consider the various aspects of both before we begin training.

Taking a new puppy home and turning him loose in your house can be compared to turning a child loose in a sports arena and telling the child that the place is all his! The sheer enormity of the place would be too much for him to handle.

Instead, offer the puppy clearly defined areas where he can play, sleep, eat and live. A room of the house where the family gathers is the most obvious choice. Puppies are social animals and need to feel a part of the pack right from the start. Hearing your voice, watching you while you are doing things and smelling you nearby are all positive reinforcers that he is now a member of your pack. Usually a family room, the kitchen or a nearby adjoining breakfast area is ideal for providing safety and security for both puppy and owner.

Within that room there should be a smaller area that the puppy can call his own. An alcove, a wire or fibreglass dog crate or a fenced (not boarded!) corner from which he can view the activities of his new family will be fine. The size of the area or crate is the key factor here. The area must be large enough for the puppy to lie down and stretch out as well as stand up without rubbing his head on the top, yet small enough so that he cannot relieve himself at one end and sleep at the other without coming into contact with his droppings until fully trained to relieve himself outside.

Dogs are, by nature, clean animals and will not remain close to their relief areas unless forced to do so. In those cases, they then become dirty dogs and usually remain that way for life.

The designated area should contain clean bedding and a toy. Water must always be available, in a non-spill container.

CONTROL

By control, we mean helping the puppy to create a lifestyle pattern that will be compatible to that of his human pack (YOU!). Just as we guide little children to learn our way of life, we must show the puppy when it is time to play, eat, sleep, exercise and even entertain himself.

105

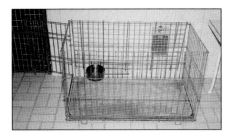

A wire crate provides the puppy with suitable ventilation and a good view of the family. During housebreaking, do not keep a water bowl inside the crate.

THE SUCCESS METHOD

Success that comes by luck is usually short lived. Success that comes by well-thought-out proven methods is often more easily achieved and permanent. This is the Success Method. It is designed to give you, the puppy owner, a simple yet proven way to help your puppy develop clean living habits and a feeling of security in his new environment.

Your puppy should always sleep in his crate. He should also learn that, during times of household confusion and excessive human activity such as at breakfast when family members are preparing for the day, he can play by himself in relative safety and comfort in his designated area. Each time you leave the

THE SUCCESS METHOD

1 Tell the puppy 'Crate time!' and place him in the crate with a small treat (a piece of cheese or half of a biscuit). Let him stay in the crate for five minutes while you are in the same room. Then release him and praise lavishly. Never release him when he is fussing. Wait until he is quiet before you let him out.

2 Repeat Step 1 several times a day.

3 The next day, place the puppy in the crate as before. Let him stay there for ten minutes. Do this several times.

4 Continue building time in five-minute increments until the puppy stays in his crate for 30 minutes with you in the room. Always take him to his relief area after prolonged periods in his crate.

5 Now go back to Step 1 and let the puppy stay in his crate for five minutes, this time while you are out of the room.

6 Once again, build crate time in five-minute increments with you out of the room. When the puppy will stay willingly in his crate (he may even fall asleep!) for 30 minutes with you out of the room, he will be ready to stay in it for several hours at a time.

6 Steps to Successful Crate Training

HOW MANY TIMES A DAY?

AGE	RELIEF TRIPS
To 14 weeks	10
14–22 weeks	8
22–32 weeks	6
Adulthood	4
(dog stops growing)	

These are estimates, of course, but they are a guide to the MINIMUM opportunities a dog should have each day to relieve itself.

puppy alone, he should understand exactly where he is to stay. Puppies are chewers. They cannot tell the difference between lamp cords, television wires, shoes, table legs, etc. Chewing into a television wire, for example, can be fatal to the puppy while a shorted wire can start a fire in the house.

If the puppy chews on the arm of the chair when he is alone, you will probably discipline him angrily when you get home. Thus, he makes the association that your coming home means he is going to be punished. (He will not remember chewing the chair and is incapable of making the association of the discipline with his naughty deed.)

Other times of excitement, such as family parties, etc., can be fun for the puppy providing he can view the activities from the security of his designated area. He is not underfoot and he is not

being fed all sorts of titbits that will probably cause him stomach distress, yet he still feels a part of the fun.

SCHEDULE

A puppy should be taken to his relief area each time he is released from his designated area, after meals, after a play session and when he first awakens in the morning (at age eight weeks, this can mean 5 a.m.!). The puppy will indicate that he's ready 'to go' by circling or sniffing busily—do not

HONOUR AND OBEY

Dogs are the most honourable animals in existence. They consider another species (humans) as their own. They interface with you. You are their leader. Puppies perceive children to be on their level; their actions around small children are different from their behaviour around their adult masters.

PLAN TO PLAY

The puppy should also have regular play and exercise sessions when he is with you or a family member. Exercise for a very young puppy can consist of a short walk around the house or garden. Playing can include fetching games with a large ball or a special raggy. (All puppies teethe and need soft things upon which to chew.) Remember to restrict play periods to indoors within his living area (the family room, for example) until he is completely housetrained.

misinterpret these signs. For a puppy less than ten weeks of age, a routine of taking him out every hour is necessary. As the puppy grows, he will be able to wait for longer periods of time.

Keep trips to his relief area short. Stay no more than five or six minutes and then return to the house. If he goes during that time, praise him lavishly and take him indoors immediately. If he does not, but he has an accident when you go back indoors, pick him up immediately, say 'No! No!' and return to his relief area. Wait a few minutes, then return to the house again. Never hit a puppy or rub his face in urine or excrement when he has had an accident!

Once indoors, put the puppy in his crate until you have had time to clean up his accident. Then release him to the family area and watch him more closely than before. Chances are, his accident was a result of your not picking up his signal or waiting too long before offering him the opportunity to relieve himself. Never hold a grudge against the puppy for accidents.

Let the puppy learn that going outdoors means it is time to relieve himself, not play. Once

PAPER CAPER

Never line your pup's sleeping area with newspaper. Puppy litters are usually raised on newspaper and, once in your home, the puppy will immediately associate newspaper with voiding. Never put newspaper on any floor while housetraining, as this will only confuse the puppy. If you are paper-training him, use paper in his designated relief area ONLY. Finally, restrict water intake after evening meals. Offer a few licks at a time—never let a young puppy gulp water after meals.

trained, he will be able to play indoors and out and still differentiate between the times for play versus the times for relief.

Help him develop regular hours for naps, being alone, playing by himself and just resting, all in his crate. Encourage him to entertain himself while you are busy with your activities. Let him learn that having you near is comforting, but it is not your main purpose in life to provide him with undivided attention.

Each time you put a puppy in his own area, use the same command, whatever suits best. Soon he will run to his crate or special area when he hears you say those words.

Crate training provides safety for you, the puppy and the home. It also provides the puppy with a

Always clean up after your dog whether you are in a public place or in your own garden.

feeling of security, and that helps the puppy achieve self-confidence and clean habits.

Remember that one of the primary ingredients in housetraining your puppy is control. Regardless of your lifestyle, there will always be occasions when you will need to have a place where your dog can stay and be happy and safe. Crate training is the answer for now and in the future.

In conclusion, a few key elements are really all you need for a successful house training method—consistency, frequency, praise, control and supervision. By following these procedures with a normal, healthy puppy, you and the puppy will soon be past the stage of 'accidents' and ready to move on to a full and rewarding life together.

ROLES OF DISCIPLINE, REWARD AND PUNISHMENT
Discipline, training one to act in accordance with rules, brings order to life. It is as simple as that. Without discipline, particu-

THE CLEAN LIFE
By providing sleeping and resting quarters that fit the dog, and offering frequent opportunities to relieve himself outside his quarters, the puppy quickly learns that the outdoors (or the newspaper if you are training him to paper) is the place to go when he needs to urinate or defecate. It also reinforces his innate desire to keep his sleeping quarters clean. This, in turn, helps develop the muscle control that will eventually produce a dog with clean living habits.

109

Your puppy will need a few toilet walks per day. Family members should take turns with the puppy so that the children and the adults share the responsibility.

larly in a group society, chaos reigns supreme and the group will eventually perish. Humans and canines are social animals and need some form of discipline in order to function effectively. They must procure food, protect their home base and their young and reproduce to keep the species going.

If there were no discipline in the lives of social animals, they would eventually die from starvation and/or predation by other stronger animals.

In the case of domestic canines, dogs need discipline in their lives in order to understand how their pack (you and other family members) functions and how they must act in order to survive.

A large humane society in a highly populated area recently surveyed dog owners regarding their satisfaction with their relationships with their dogs. People who had trained their dogs were 75% more satisfied with their pets than those who had never trained their dogs.

Dr Edward Thorndike, a psychologist, established *Thorndike's Theory of Learning*, which states that a behaviour that results in a pleasant event tends to be repeated. A behaviour that results in an unpleasant event tends not to be repeated. It is this theory on which training methods are based today. For example, if you manipulate a dog to perform a specific behaviour and reward him for doing it, he is likely to do it again because he enjoyed the end result.

Occasionally, punishment, a penalty inflicted for an offence, is necessary. The best type of punishment often comes from an outside source. For example, a child is told not to touch the stove because he may get burned. He disobeys and touches the stove. In doing so, he receives a burn. From that time on, he respects the heat of the stove and avoids contact with it. Therefore, a behaviour that results in an unpleasant event tends not to be repeated.

A good example of a dog learning the hard way is the dog who chases the house cat. He is told many times to leave the cat alone, yet he persists in teasing the cat. Then, one day he begins chasing the cat but the cat turns and swipes a claw across the dog's face, leaving him with a painful gash on his nose. The final result is that the dog stops chasing the cat.

TAKE THE LEAD
Do not carry your dog to his toilet area. Lead him there on a leash or, better yet, encourage him to follow you to the spot. If you start carrying him to his spot, you might end up doing this routine forever and your dog will have the satisfaction of having trained YOU.

Belgians do not outgrow their need to play until well into their senior years. This Malinois is initiating play with his owner.

TRAINING EQUIPMENT

Collar and Lead

For a Belgian Shepherd the collar and lead that you use for training must be one with which you are easily able to work, not too heavy for the dog and perfectly safe.

Treats

Have a bag of treats on hand. Something nutritious and easy to swallow works best. Use a soft treat, a chunk of cheese or a piece of cooked chicken rather than a dry biscuit. By the time the dog has finished chewing a dry treat, he will forget why he is being rewarded in the first place! Using food rewards will not teach a dog to beg at the table—the only way to teach a dog to beg at the table is to give him food from the table. In training, rewarding the dog with a food treat will help him associate praise and the treats with learning new behaviours that obviously please his owner.

TRAINING BEGINS: ASK THE DOG A QUESTION

In order to teach your dog anything, you must first get his attention. After all, he cannot learn anything if he is looking away from you with his mind on something else.

To get his attention, ask him, 'School?' and immediately walk over to him and give him a treat as you tell him 'Good dog.' Wait a minute or two and repeat the routine, this time with a treat in your hand as you approach within a foot of the dog. Do not go directly to him, but stop about a foot short of him and hold out the treat as you ask, 'School?' He will see you approaching with a treat in your hand and most likely begin walking toward you. As you meet, give him the treat and praise again.

The third time, ask the question, have a treat in your hand and walk only a short distance toward the dog so that he must walk almost all the way to you. As he reaches you, give him the treat and praise again.

By this time, the dog will probably be getting the idea that if he pays attention to you, especially when you ask that question, it will pay off in treats and enjoyable activities for him. In other words, he learns that 'school' means doing great things with you that are fun and result in positive attention for him.

Remember that the dog does not understand your verbal language; he only recognises sounds. Your question translates to a series of sounds for him, and those sounds become the signal to go to you and pay attention; if he

THE GOLDEN RULE

The golden rule of dog training is simple. For each 'question' (command), there is only one correct answer (reaction). One command = one reaction. Keep practising the command until the dog reacts correctly without hesitating. Be repetitive but not monotonous. Dogs get bored just as people do!

'NO' MEANS 'NO!'

Dogs do not understand our language. They can be trained to react to a certain sound, at a certain volume. If you say 'No, Oliver' in a very soft pleasant voice it will not have the same meaning as 'No, Oliver!!' when you shout it as loud as you can. You should never use the dog's name during a reprimand, just the command NO!! Since dogs don't understand words, comics often use dogs trained with opposite meanings. Thus, when the comic commands his dog to SIT the dog will stand up, and vice versa.

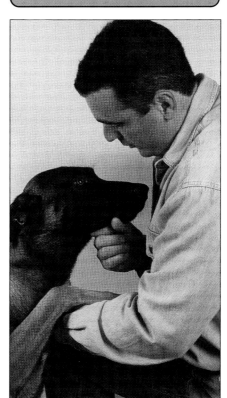

A properly trained Belgian Shepherd will want to please you in his every action. Intelligent dogs like these rarely need scolding or correction.

Your dog must be trained. The SIT command should be one of the first lessons for both you and the dog to learn.

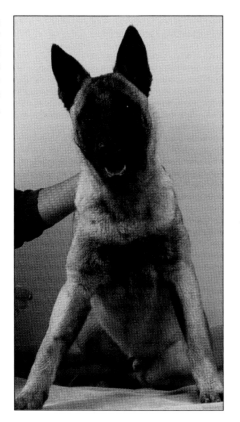

does, he will get to interact with you plus receive treats and praise.

THE BASIC COMMANDS

TEACHING SIT

Now that you have the dog's attention, attach his lead and hold it in your left hand and a food treat in your right. Place your food hand at the dog's nose and let him lick the treat but not take it from you. Say 'Sit' and slowly raise your food hand from in front of the dog's nose up over his head so

that he is looking at the ceiling. As he bends his head upward, he will have to bend his knees to maintain his balance. As he bends his knees, he will assume a sit position. At that point, release the food treat and praise lavishly with comments such as 'Good dog! Good sit!,' etc. Remember to always praise enthusiastically, because dogs relish verbal praise from their owners and feel so proud of themselves whenever they accomplish a behaviour.

You will not use food forever in getting the dog to obey your commands. Food is only used to teach new behaviours, and once the dog knows what you want when you give a specific command, you will wean him off the food treats but still maintain the verbal praise. After all, you will always have your voice with you, and there will be many times when you have no food rewards but expect the dog to obey.

TEACHING DOWN

Teaching the down exercise is easy when you understand how the dog perceives the down position, and it is very difficult when you do not. Dogs perceive the down position as a submissive one, therefore teaching the down exercise using a forceful method can sometimes make the dog develop such a fear of the down that he either runs away when you say 'Down' or he attempts to snap at the person who tries to force him down.

Have the dog sit close alongside your left leg, facing in the same direction as you are. Hold the lead in your left hand and a food treat in your right. Now place your left hand lightly on the top of the dog's shoulders where they meet above the spinal cord. Do not push down on the dog's shoulders; simply rest your left hand there so you can guide the dog to lie down close to your left leg rather than to swing away from your side when he drops.

Now place the food hand at the dog's nose, say 'Down' very softly (almost a whisper), and slowly lower the food hand to the dog's front feet. When the food hand reaches the floor, begin moving it forward along the floor in front of the dog. Keep talking softly to the dog, saying things like, 'Do you want this treat? You can do this, good dog.' Your reassuring tone of voice will help calm the dog as he tries to follow the food hand in order to get the treat.

When the dog's elbows touch the floor, release the food and

DOUBLE JEOPARDY

A dog in jeopardy never lies down. He stays alert on his feet because instinct tells him that he may have to run away or fight for his survival. Therefore, if a dog feels threatened or anxious, he will not lie down. Consequently, it is important to have the dog calm and relaxed as he learns the down exercise.

The COME exercise should not be frightening for the dog or it will never be effective.

OPEN MINDS

Dogs are as different from each other as people are. What works for one dog may not work for another. Have an open mind. If one method of training is unsuccessful, try another.

praise softly. Try to get the dog to maintain that down position for several seconds before you let him sit up again. The goal here is to get the dog to settle down and not feel threatened in the down position.

FEAR AGGRESSION

Pups who are subjected to physical abuse during training commonly end up with behavioural problems as adults. One common result of abuse is fear aggression, in which a dog will lash out, bare his teeth, snarl and finally bite someone by whom he feels threatened. For example, your daughter may be playing with the dog one afternoon. As they play hide-and-seek, she backs the dog into a corner, and as she attempts to tease him playfully, he bites her hand. Examine the cause of this behaviour. Did your daughter ever hit the dog? Did someone who resembles your daughter hit or scream at the dog? Fortunately, fear aggression is relatively easy to correct. Have your daughter engage in only positive activities with the dog, such as feeding, petting and walking. She should not give any corrections or negative feedback. If the dog still growls or cowers away from her, allow someone else to accompany them. After approximately one week, the dog should feel that he can rely on her for many positive things, and he will also be prevented from reacting fearfully towards anyone who might resemble her.

TEACHING STAY

It is easy to teach the dog to stay in either a sit or a down position. Again, we use food and praise during the teaching process as we help the dog to understand exactly what it is that we are expecting him to do.

To teach the sit/stay, start with the dog sitting on your left side as before and hold the lead in your left hand. Have a food treat in your right hand and place your food hand at the dog's nose. Say 'Stay' and step out on your right foot to stand directly in front of the dog, toe to toe, as he licks and nibbles the treat. Be sure to keep his head facing upward to maintain the sit position. Count to five and then swing around to stand next to the dog again with him on your left. As soon as you get back to the original position, release the food and praise lavishly.

To teach the down/stay, do the down as previously described. As soon as the dog lies down, say 'Stay' and step out on your right foot just as you did in the sit/stay. Count to five and then return to stand beside the dog with him on your left side. Release the treat and praise as always.

Within a week or ten days, you can begin to add a bit of distance between you and your dog when you leave him. When you do, use your left hand open with the palm facing the dog as a stay signal, much the same as the hand signal a constable uses to stop traffic at an intersection. Hold the food treat in your right hand as before, but this time the food is not touching the dog's nose. He will watch the food hand and quickly learn that he is going to get that treat as soon as you return to his side.

When you can stand 1 metre away from your dog for 30 seconds, you can then begin building time and distance in both stays. Eventually, the dog can be expected to remain in the stay position for prolonged periods of time until you return to him or call him to you. Always praise lavishly when he stays.

TEACHING COME

If you make teaching 'come' an exciting experience, you should never have a 'student' that does not love the game or that fails to come when called. The secret, it seems, is never to teach the word 'come.'

At times when an owner most wants his dog to come when called, the owner is likely to be upset or anxious and he allows these feelings to come through in

the tone of his voice when he calls his dog. Hearing that desperation in his owner's voice, the dog fears the results of going to him and therefore either disobeys outright or runs in the opposite direction. The secret, therefore, is to teach the dog a game and, when you want him to come to you, simply play the game. It is practically a no-fail solution!

To begin, have several members of your family take a few food treats and each go into a different room in the house. Take turns calling the dog, and each person should celebrate the dog's

STAY is a relatively simple exercise to teach your dog. Combine the STAY exercise with the DOWN command.

'COME' . . . BACK

Never call your dog to come to you for a correction or scold him when he reaches you. That is the quickest way to turn a 'Come' command into 'Go away fast!' Dogs think only in the present tense, and your dog will connect the scolding with coming to you, not with the misbehaviour of a few moments earlier.

old companion dog who went blind, but who never fails to locate her owner when asked, 'Where are you?'

Children, in particular, love to play this game with their dogs. Children can hide in smaller places like a shower or bath, behind a bed or under a table. The dog needs to work a little bit harder to find these hiding places, but when he does he loves to celebrate with a treat and a tussle with a favourite youngster.

finding him with a treat and lots of happy praise. When a person calls the dog, he is actually inviting the dog to find him and get a treat as a reward for 'winning.'

A few turns of the 'Where are you?' game and the dog will understand that everyone is playing the game and that each person has a big celebration awaiting his success at locating them. Once he learns to love the game, simply calling out 'Where are you?' will bring him running from wherever he is when he hears that all-important question.

The come command is recognised as one of the most important things to teach a dog, but there are trainers who work with thousands of dogs and never teach the actual word 'Come.' Yet these dogs will race to respond to a person who uses the dog's name followed by 'Where are you?' For example, a woman has a 12-year-

TEACHING HEEL

Heeling means that the dog walks beside the owner without pulling. It takes time and patience on the owner's part to succeed at teaching the dog that he (the owner) will not proceed unless the dog is walking calmly beside him. Pulling out ahead on the lead is definitely not acceptable.

Begin by holding the lead in your left hand as the dog sits beside your left leg. Move the loop end of the lead to your right hand but keep your left hand short on the lead so it keeps the dog in close next to you.

COMMAND STANCE

Stand up straight and authoritatively when giving your dog commands. Do not issue commands when lying on the floor or lying on your back on the sofa. If you are on your hands and knees when you give a command, your dog will think you are positioning yourself to play.

Say 'Heel' and step forward on your left foot. Keep the dog close to you and take three steps. Stop and have the dog sit next to you in what we now call the 'heel position.' Praise verbally, but do not touch the dog. Hesitate a moment and begin again with 'Heel,' taking three steps and stopping, at which point the dog is told to sit again.

Your goal here is to have the dog walk those three steps without pulling on the lead. Once he will walk calmly beside you for three steps without pulling, increase the number of steps you take to five. When he will walk

KEEP SMILING

Never train your dog, puppy or adult, when you are angry or in a sour mood. Dogs are very sensitive to human feelings, especially anger, and if your dog senses that you are angry or upset, he will connect your anger with his training and learn to resent or fear his training sessions.

politely beside you while you take five steps, you can increase the length of your walk to ten steps. Keep increasing the length of your stroll until the dog will walk quietly beside you without pulling as long as you want him to heel. When you stop heeling, indicate to the dog that the exercise is over by verbally praising as you pet him and say 'OK, good dog.' The 'OK' is used as a release word meaning that the exercise is finished and the dog is free to relax.

Once your Belgian Shepherd has mastered all the basic commands, you should review the commands, in various sequences, for the duration of the dog's life.

119

Belgian Shepherd Dog

You must train your dog to HEEL so it can walk properly alongside you, sitting when you stop walking.

TUG OF WALK?

If you begin teaching the heel by taking long walks and letting the dog pull you along, he misinterprets this action as an acceptable form of taking a walk. When you pull back on the lead to counteract his pulling, he reads that tug as a signal to pull even harder!

Be certain you have your dog's undivided attention before proceeding with the lesson.

If you are dealing with a dog who insists on pulling you around, simply 'put on your brakes' and stand your ground until the dog realises that the two of you are not going anywhere until he is beside you and moving at your pace, not his. It may take some time just standing there to convince the dog that you are the leader and you will be the one to decide on the direction and speed of your travel.

Each time the dog looks up at you or slows down to give a slack lead between the two of you, quietly praise him and say, 'Good heel. Good dog.' Eventually, the dog will begin to respond and within a few days he will be walking politely beside you

without pulling on the lead. At first, the training sessions should be kept short and very positive; soon the dog will be able to walk nicely with you for increasingly

Heeling is the most important command to teach a show dog, who has to exhibit his proper gait to the judge.

TAKING CONTROL

If you are walking your dog and he suddenly stops and looks straight into your eyes, ignore him. Pull the leash and lead him into the direction you want to walk.

HEELING WELL

Teach your dog to HEEL in an enclosed area. Once you think the dog will obey reliably and you want to attempt advanced obedience exercises such as off-lead heeling, test him in a fenced-in area so he cannot run away.

OBEDIENCE CLASSES

It is a good idea to enrol in an obedience class if one is available in your area. If yours is a show dog, ringcraft classes would be more appropriate. Many areas have dog clubs that offer basic obedience training as well as preparatory classes for obedience competition. There are also local dog trainers who offer similar classes.

At obedience trials, dogs can earn titles at various levels of competition. The beginning levels of competition include basic behaviours such as sit, down, heel, etc. The more advanced levels of competition include jumping, retrieving, scent discrimination and signal work. The advanced levels require a dog and owner to put a lot of time and effort into their training and the

longer distances. Remember also to give the dog free time and the opportunity to run and play when you have finished heel practice.

WEANING OFF FOOD IN TRAINING

Food is used in training new behaviours. Once the dog understands what behaviour goes with a specific command, it is time to start weaning him off the food treats. At first, give a treat after each exercise. Then, start to give a treat only after every other exercise. Mix up the times when you offer a food reward and the times when you only offer praise so that the dog will never know when he is going to receive both food and praise and when he is going to receive only praise. This is called a variable ratio reward system and it proves successful because there is always the chance that the owner will produce a treat, so the dog never stops trying for that reward. No matter what, ALWAYS give verbal praise.

DID YOU KNOW?

Occasionally, a dog and owner who have not attended formal classes have been able to earn entry-level titles by obtaining competition rules and regulations from a local kennel club and practising on their own to a degree of perfection. Obtaining the higher level titles, however, almost always requires extensive training under the tutelage of experienced instructors. In addition, the more difficult levels require more specialised equipment whereas the lower levels do not.

titles that can be earned at these levels of competition are very prestigious.

OTHER ACTIVITIES FOR LIFE

Whether a dog is trained in the structured environment of a class or alone with his owner at home, there are many activities that can bring fun and rewards to both owner and dog once they have mastered basic control.

Teaching the dog to help out around the home, in the garden or on the farm provides great satisfaction to both dog and owner. In addition, the dog's help makes life a little easier for his owner and raises his stature as a valued companion to his family. It helps give the dog a purpose by occupying his mind and providing an outlet for his energy.

Backpacking is an exciting and healthy activity that the dog can be taught without assistance from more than his owner. The exercise of walking and climbing is good for man and dog alike, and the bond that they develop together is priceless. The rule for backpacking with any dog is never to expect the dog to carry more than one-sixth of his body weight.

If you are interested in participating in organised competition with your Belgian Shepherd, there are activities other than obedience in which you and your dog can become involved.

DOG SHOWS

If you are interested in exploring dog shows, your best bet is to join your local breed club. These clubs often host both Championship and Open Shows, and sometimes Match meetings and special events, all of which could be of

interest, even if you are only an onlooker. To locate the breed club closest to you, contact The Kennel Club, the ruling body for the British dog world. The Kennel Club governs not only conformation shows but also working trials, obedience trials, agility trials and field trials. The Kennel Club furnishes the rules and regulations for all these events plus general dog registration and other basic requirements of dog ownership. Its annual show, called the Crufts Dog Show, held in Birmingham, is

Agility trials provide a wonderful outlet for the well-trained athlete. Belgian Shepherds prove most successful in these trials.

Belgian Shepherd Dogs are naturally agile and coordinated, showing off their skills in the most difficult of agility events.

it's fun to do, fun to watch and great exercise.

SCHUTZHUND

As a Belgian Shepherd owner, you have the opportunity to participate in Schutzhund competition if you choose. Schutzhund originated as a test to determine the best quality Belgian Shepherds to be used for breeding stock. Breeders continue to use it as a way to evaluate working

the largest benched show in England. Every year over 20,000 of the UK's best dogs qualify to participate in this marvellous show which lasts four days.

AGILITY TRIALS

Agility is a popular sport where dogs run through an obstacle course that includes various jumps, tunnels and other exercises to test the dog's speed and coordination. The owners run beside their dogs to give commands and to guide them through the course. Although competitive, the focus is on fun—

ability and temperament. There are three levels in Schutzhund trials: SchH I, SchH II and SchH III, with each level being progressively more difficult to complete successfully. Each level consists of training, obedience and protection phases. Training for Schutzhund is intense and must be practised consistently to keep the dog keen. The experience of Schutzhund training is very rewarding for dog and owner, and the Belgian Shepherd's tractability is well suited for this type of training.

HERDING TESTS AND TRIALS

Belgian Shepherds were originally bred for herding, a precious natural ability. They were expected to protect their flock and farm. They worked not only sheep but also dairy cattle, goats, swine, etc.

When a Belgian Shepherd Dog fancier is curious to know whether his Belgian retained the herding instincts of the breed, his

dog can take the Herding Instinct Test. This test also makes it possible for breeders to select for this important natural instinct that may not be lost in the breed.

Herding dog competitions have existed as long as shepherds have been using dogs. Today Belgian Shepherds can compete in trials in which sheep and cattle are used. All over the United Kingdom, trials are held under the rules of the International Sheepdog Society. There are herding trials for both novice and experienced competitors. They are organised by many associations and are mostly open to all breeds. The tools of the handlers of shepherding are the whistle, the voice and the crook or stick. Belgian Shepherd owners find these trials the most exciting of all events in which to participate, and the audiences are immensely enthusiastic. In the UK many trials are televised to even larger audiences.

Schutzhund is a form of protection work in which Belgian Shepherds excel. The man in the bite suit is agitating the dog to gauge his courage and strength.

OBEDIENCE SCHOOL

Taking your dog to an obedience school may be the best investment in time and money you can ever make. You will enjoy the benefits for the lifetime of your dog and you will have the opportunity to meet people with your similar expectations for companion dogs.

125

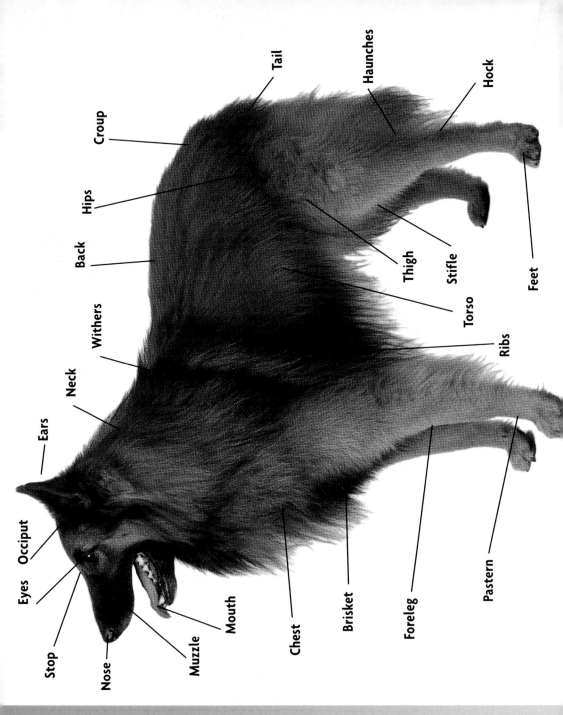

Tail

Haunches

Hock

Croup

Hips

Back

Thigh

Stifle

Torso

Feet

Withers

Ribs

Neck

Ears

Occiput

Eyes

Stop

Nose

Muzzle

Mouth

Chest

Brisket

Foreleg

Pastern

Physical Structure of the Belgian Shepherd Dog

Dogs suffer from many of the same physical illnesses as people. They might even share many of the same psychological problems. Since people usually know more about human diseases than canine maladies, many of the terms used in this chapter will be familiar but not necessarily those used by veterinary surgeons. We will use the term *x-ray*, instead of the more acceptable term *radiograph*. We will also use the familiar term *symptoms* even though dogs don't have symptoms, which are verbal descriptions of the patient's feelings; dogs have *clinical signs*. Since dogs can't speak, we have to look for clinical signs...but we still use the term symptoms in this book.

As a general rule, medicine is practised. That term is not arbitrary. Medicine is a constantly changing art as we learn more and more about genetics, electronic aids (like CAT scans) and daily laboratory advances. There are many dog maladies, like canine hip dysplasia, which are not universally treated in the same manner. Some veterinary surgeons

opt for surgery more often than others do.

SELECTING A VETERINARY SURGEON

Your selection of a veterinary surgeon should not be based upon personality (as most are) but upon their convenience to your home. You want a vet who is close because you might have emergencies or need to make multiple visits for treatments. You want a vet who has services that you might require such as tattooing and grooming, as well as sophisticated pet supplies and a good reputation for ability and responsiveness. There is nothing more frustrating than having to wait a day or more to get a response

Before you buy a dog, meet and interview the veterinary surgeons in your area. Take everything into consideration; discuss background, specialities, fees, emergency policies, etc.

1. Esophagus
2. Lungs
3. Gall Bladder
4. Liver
5. Kidney
6. Stomach
7. Intestines
8. Urinary Bladder

Internal Organs of the Belgian Shepherd Dog

from your veterinary surgeon.

All veterinary surgeons are licensed and their diplomas and/or certificates should be displayed in their waiting rooms. There are, however, many veterinary specialities that usually require further studies and internships. There are specialists in heart problems (veterinary cardiologists), skin problems (veterinary dermatologists), teeth and gum problems (veterinary dentists), eye problems (veterinary ophthalmologists) and x-rays (veterinary radiologists), as well as vets who have specialities in bones, muscles or other organs. Most veterinary surgeons do routine surgery such as neutering, stitching up wounds and docking tails for those breeds in which such is required for show purposes. When the problem affecting your dog is serious, it is not unusual or impudent to get another medical opinion, although in Britain you are obliged to advise the vets concerned about this. You might also want to compare costs among several veterinary surgeons. Sophisticated health care and veterinary services can be very costly. Important decisions are often based upon financial considerations.

PREVENTATIVE MEDICINE

It is much easier, less costly and more effective to practise preven-

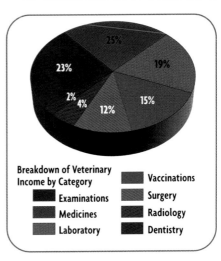

Breakdown of Veterinary Income by Category

- Examinations
- Medicines
- Laboratory
- Vaccinations
- Surgery
- Radiology
- Dentistry

A typical American vet's income, categorised according to services provided. This survey dealt with small-animal practices.

tative medicine than to fight bouts of illness and disease. Properly bred puppies come from parents who were selected based upon their genetic disease profile. Their mothers should have been vaccinated, free of all internal and external parasites and properly nourished. For these reasons, a visit to the veterinary surgeon who cared for the dam is recommended. The dam can pass on disease resistance to her puppies, which can last for eight to ten weeks. She can also pass on parasites and many infections. That's why you should visit the veterinary surgeon who cared for the dam.

VACCINATION SCHEDULING

Most vaccinations are given by injection and should only be done by a veterinary surgeon. Both he and you should keep a record of

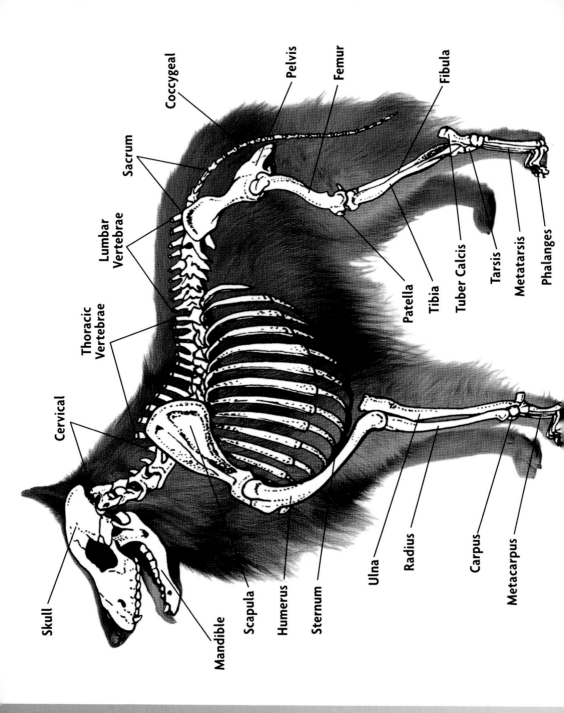

Coccygeal

Pelvis

Femur

Fibula

Sacrum

Lumbar Vertebrae

Patella

Tibia

Tuber Calcis

Tarsis

Metatarsis

Phalanges

Thoracic Vertebrae

Cervical

Skull

Mandible

Scapula

Humerus

Sternum

Ulna

Radius

Carpus

Metacarpus

Skeletal Structure of the Belgian Shepherd Dog

the date of the injection, the identification of the vaccine and the amount given. Some vets give a first vaccination at eight weeks, but most dog breeders prefer the course not to commence until about ten weeks because of negating any antibodies passed on by the dam. The vaccination scheduling is usually based on a 15-day cycle. You must take your vet's advice regarding when to vaccinate as this may differ according to the vaccine used. Most vaccinations immunize your puppy against viruses.

The usual vaccines contain immunizing doses of several different viruses such as distemper, parvovirus, parainfluenza and hepatitis although some veterinary surgeons recommend separate vaccines for each disease. There are other vaccines available when the puppy is at risk. You should rely upon professional advice. This is especially true for the booster-shot programme. Most vaccination

MORE THAN VACCINES
Vaccinations help prevent your new puppy from contracting diseases, but they do not cure them. Proper nutrition as well as parasite control keep your dog healthy and less susceptible to many dangerous diseases. Remember that your dog depends on you to ensure his well-being.

programmes require a booster when the puppy is a year old and once a year thereafter. In some cases, circumstances may require more or less frequent immunizations. Kennel cough, more formally known as tracheobronchitis, is treated with a vaccine that is sprayed into the dog's nostrils. Kennel cough is usually included in routine vaccination, but this is often not so effective as for other major diseases.

WEANING TO FIVE MONTHS OLD
Puppies should be weaned by the time they are about two months old. A puppy that remains for at least eight weeks with its mother and littermates usually adapts better to other dogs and people later in its life.

Some new owners have their puppy examined by a veterinary surgeon immediately, which is a good idea. Vaccination programmes usually begin when the puppy is very young.

The puppy will have its teeth examined and have its skeletal conformation and general health checked prior to certification by the veterinary surgeon. Puppies in certain breeds have problems with their kneecaps, cataracts and other eye problems, heart murmurs and undescended testicles. They may also have personality problems and your veterinary surgeon might have training in temperament evaluation.

Normal hairs of a dog enlarged 200 times original size. The cuticle (outer covering) is clean and healthy. Unlike human hair that grows from the base, a dog's hair also grows from the end, as shown in the inset. Scanning electron micrographs by Dr Dennis Kunkel, University of Hawaii.

FIVE TO TWELVE MONTHS OF AGE

Unless you intend to breed or show your dog, neutering the puppy at six months of age is recommended. Discuss this with your veterinary surgeon. Neutering has proven to be extremely beneficial to both male and female puppies. Besides eliminating the possibility of pregnancy, it inhibits (but does not prevent) breast cancer in bitches and prostate cancer in male dogs. Under no circumstances should a bitch be spayed prior to her first season.

Your veterinary surgeon should provide your puppy with a thorough dental evaluation at six months of age, ascertaining whether all the permanent teeth have erupted properly. A home dental care regimen should be initiated at six months, including brushing weekly and providing good dental devices (such as nylon bones). Regular dental care promotes healthy teeth, fresh breath and a longer life.

ONE TO SEVEN YEARS

Once a year, your grown dog should visit the vet for an examination and vaccination boosters, if needed. Some vets recommend blood tests, thyroid level check and dental evaluation to accompany these annual visits. A thorough clinical evaluation by the vet can provide critical background information for your

DENTAL HEALTH

A dental examination is in order when the dog is between six months and one year of age so any permanent teeth that have erupted incorrectly can be corrected. It is important to begin a brushing routine, preferably using a two-sided brushing technique, whereby both sides of the tooth are brushed at the same time. Durable nylon and safe edible chews should be a part of your puppy's arsenal for good health, good teeth and pleasant breath. The vast majority of dogs three to four years old and older have diseases of the gums from lack of dental attention. Using the various types of dental chews can be very effective in controlling dental plaque.

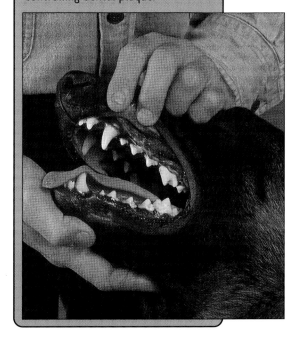

HEALTH AND VACCINATION SCHEDULE

AGE IN WEEKS:	6TH	8TH	10TH	12TH	14TH	16TH	20-24TH	1 YR
Worm Control	✔	✔	✔	✔	✔	✔	✔	
Neutering								✔
Heartworm*		✔		✔		✔	✔	
Parvovirus	✔		✔		✔		✔	✔
Distemper		✔		✔		✔		✔
Hepatitis		✔		✔		✔		✔
Leptospirosis								✔
Parainfluenza	✔		✔		✔			✔
Dental Examination		✔					✔	✔
Complete Physical		✔					✔	✔
Coronavirus				✔			✔	✔
Kennel Cough	✔							
Hip Dysplasia								✔
Rabies*							✔	

Vaccinations are not instantly effective. It takes about two weeks for the dog's immunization system to develop antibodies. Most vaccinations require annual booster shots. Your veterinary surgeon should guide you in this regard.
*Not applicable in the United Kingdom

dog. Blood tests are often performed at one year of age, and dental examinations around the third or fourth birthday. In the long run, quality preventative care for your pet can save money, teeth and lives.

SKIN PROBLEMS IN BELGIAN SHEPHERDS
Veterinary surgeons are consulted by dog owners for skin problems more than any other group of diseases or maladies. Dogs' skin is almost as sensitive as human skin and both suffer almost the same ailments (though the occurrence of acne in dogs is rare!). For this reason, veterinary dermatology has developed into a speciality practised by many veterinary surgeons.

Since many skin problems have visual symptoms that are almost identical, it requires the skill of an experienced veterinary dermatologist to identify and cure many of the more severe skin disorders. Pet shops sell many treatments for skin problems but most of the treatments are directed at symptoms and not the underlying problem(s). If your dog is suffering from a skin disorder, you should seek professional assistance as quickly as possible.

As with all diseases, the earlier a problem is identified and treated, the more successful is the cure.

HEREDITARY SKIN DISORDERS

Veterinary dermatologists are currently researching a number of skin disorders that are believed to have a hereditary basis. These inherited diseases are transmitted by both parents, who appear (phenotypically) normal but have a recessive gene for the disease, meaning that they carry, but are not affected by, the disease. These diseases pose serious problems to breeders because in some instances there is no method of identifying carriers. Often the secondary diseases associated with these skin conditions are even more debilitating than the disorder itself, including cancers and respiratory problems; others can be lethal.

Among the hereditary skin disorders, for which the mode of inheritance is known, are: acrodermatitis, cutaneous asthenia (Ehlers-Danlos syndrome),

DISEASE REFERENCE CHART

	What is it?	What causes it?	Symptoms
Leptospirosis	Severe disease that affects the internal organs; can be spread to people.	A bacterium, which is often carried by rodents, that enters through mucous membranes and spreads quickly throughout the body.	Range from fever, vomiting and loss of appetite in less severe cases to shock, irreversible kidney damage and possibly death in most severe cases.
Rabies	Potentially deadly virus that infects warm-blooded mammals. Not seen in United Kingdom.	Bite from a carrier of the virus, mainly wild animals.	1st stage: dog exhibits change in behaviour, fear. 2nd stage: dog's behaviour becomes more aggressive. 3rd stage: loss of coordination, trouble with bodily functions.
Parvovirus	Highly contagious virus, potentially deadly.	Ingestion of the virus, which is usually spread through the faeces of infected dogs.	Most common: severe diarrhoea. Also vomiting, fatigue, lack of appetite.
Kennel cough	Contagious respiratory infection.	Combination of types of bacteria and virus. Most common: *Bordetella bronchiseptica* bacteria and parainfluenza virus.	Chronic cough.
Distemper	Disease primarily affecting respiratory and nervous system.	Virus that is related to the human measles virus.	Mild symptoms such as fever, lack of appetite and mucous secretion progress to evidence of brain damage, 'hard pad.'
Hepatitis	Virus primarily affecting the liver.	Canine adenovirus type I (CAV-1). Enters system when dog breathes in particles.	Lesser symptoms include listlessness, diarrhoea, vomiting. More severe symptoms include 'blue-eye' (clumps of virus in eye).
Coronavirus	Virus resulting in digestive problems.	Virus is spread through infected dog's faeces.	Stomach upset evidenced by lack of appetite, vomiting, diarrhoea.

sebaceous adenitis, cyclic hematopoiesis, dermatomyositis, IgA deficiency, colour dilution alopecia and nodular dermatofibrosis. Some of these disorders are limited to one or two breeds and others affect a large number of breeds. All inherited diseases must be diagnosed and treated by a veterinary specialist.

PARASITE BITES
Many of us are allergic to insect bites. The bites itch, erupt and may even become infected. Dogs have the same reaction to fleas, ticks and/or mites. When an insect lands on you, you have the chance to whisk it away with your hand. Unfortunately, when your dog is bitten by a flea, tick or mite, it can only scratch it away or bite it. By the time the dog has

Many large-breed dogs develop a condition known as acral like granuloma. They lick a hot spot on their leg until it gets raw and infected. You should see a veterinary surgeon immediately for treatment.

been bitten, the parasite has done some of its damage. It may also have laid eggs to cause further problems in the near future. The itching from parasite bites is probably due to the saliva injected into the site when the parasite sucks the dog's blood.

AUTO-IMMUNE SKIN CONDITIONS
Auto-immune skin conditions are commonly referred to as being allergic to yourself, while allergies are usually inflammatory reactions to an outside stimulus. Auto-immune diseases cause serious damage to the tissues that are involved.

The best known auto-immune disease is lupus, which affects people as well as dogs. The symptoms are variable and may affect the kidneys, bones, blood chemistry and skin. It can be fatal to both dogs and humans, though it is not thought to be transmissible. It is usually successfully treated with cortisone, prednisone or a similar corticosteroid, but extensive use of these drugs can have harmful side effects.

ACRAL LICK GRANULOMA
Many large dogs have a very poorly understood syndrome called acral lick granuloma. The manifestation of the problem is the dog's tireless attack at a specific area of the body, almost always the legs or paws. They lick so intensely that they remove the

First Aid at a Glance

Burns
Place the affected area under cool water; use ice if only a small area is burnt.

Bee/Insect bites
Apply ice to relieve swelling; antihistamine dosed properly.

Animal bites
Clean any bleeding area; apply pressure until bleeding subsides; go to the vet.

Spider bites
Use cold compress and a pressurised pack to inhibit venom's spreading.

Antifreeze poisoning
Induce vomiting with hydrogen peroxide. Seek *immediate* veterinary help!

Fish hooks
Removal best handled by vet; hook must be cut in order to remove.

Snake bites
Pack ice around bite; contact vet quickly; identify snake for proper antivenin.

Car accident
Move dog from roadway with blanket; seek veterinary aid.

Shock
Calm the dog, keep him warm; seek immediate veterinary help.

Nosebleed
Apply cold compress to the nose; apply pressure to any visible abrasion.

Bleeding
Apply pressure above the area; treat wound by applying a cotton pack.

Heat stroke
Submerge dog in cold bath; cool down with fresh air and water; go to the vet.

Frostbite/Hypothermia
Warm the dog with a warm bath, electric blankets or hot water bottles.

Abrasions
Clean the wound and wash out thoroughly with fresh water; apply antiseptic.

 Remember: an injured dog may attempt to bite a helping hand from fear and confusion. Always muzzle the dog before trying to offer assistance.

hair and skin, leaving an ugly, large wound. Tiny protuberances, which are outgrowths of new capillaries, bead on the surface of the wound. Owners who notice their dogs' biting and chewing at their extremities should have the vet determine the cause. If lick granuloma is identified, although there is no absolute cure, corticosteroids are the most common treatment.

AIRBORNE ALLERGIES

An interesting allergy is pollen allergy. Humans have hay fever, rose fever and other fevers with which they suffer during the pollinating season. Many dogs suffer the same allergies. When the pollen count is high, your dog might suffer but don't expect him to sneeze and have a runny nose like humans. Dogs react to pollen allergies the same way they react to fleas—they scratch and bite themselves.

Dogs, like humans, can be tested for allergens. Discuss the testing with your veterinary dermatologist.

FOOD PROBLEMS

FOOD ALLERGIES

Dogs are allergic to many foods that are best-sellers and highly recommended by breeders and veterinary surgeons. Changing the brand of food that you buy may not eliminate the problem if the element to which the dog is allergic is contained in the new brand.

Recognising a food allergy is difficult. Humans vomit or have rashes when they eat a food to which they are allergic. Dogs neither vomit nor (usually) develop a rash. They react in the same manner as they do to an airborne or flea allergy; they itch, scratch and bite, thus making the diagnosis extremely difficult. While pollen allergies and parasite bites are usually seasonal, food allergies are year-round problems.

FOOD INTOLERANCE

Food intolerance is the inability of the dog to completely digest certain foods. Puppies that may have done very well on their mother's milk may not do well on cow's milk. The rest of this food intolerance may be loose bowels, passing gas and stomach pains. These are the only obvious symptoms of food intolerance and that makes diagnosis difficult.

TREATING FOOD PROBLEMS

It is possible to handle food allergies and food intolerance

THE SAME ALLERGIES

Chances are that you and your dog will have the same allergies. Your allergies are readily recognisable and usually easily treated. Your dog's allergies may be masked.

yourself. Put your dog on a diet that it has never had. Obviously if it has never eaten this new food it can't have been allergic or intolerant of it. Start with a single ingredient that is not in the dog's diet at the present time. Ingredients like chopped beef or fish are common in dogs' diets, so try something more exotic like rabbit, pheasant or even just vegetables. Keep the dog on this diet (with no additives) for a month. If the symptoms of food allergy or intolerance disappear, chances are your dog has a food allergy.

Don't think that the single ingredient cured the problem. You still must find a suitable diet and ascertain which ingredient in the old diet was objectionable. This is most easily done by adding ingredients to the new diet one at a time. Let the dog stay on the modified diet for a month before you add another ingredient. Eventually, you will determine the ingredient that caused the adverse reaction.

An alternative method is to carefully study the ingredients in the diet to which your dog is allergic or intolerant. Identify the main ingredient in this diet and eliminate the main ingredient by buying a different food that does not have that ingredient. Keep experimenting until the symptoms disappear after one month on the new diet.

CARETAKER OF TEETH

You are your dog's caretaker and his dentist. Vets warn that plaque and tartar buildup on the teeth will damage the gums and allow bacteria to enter the dog's bloodstream, causing serious damage to the animal's vital organs. Studies show that over 50 percent of dogs have some form of gum disease before age three. Daily or weekly tooth cleaning (with a brush or soft gauze pad wipes) can add years to your dog's life.

A scanning electron micrograph (S. E. M.) of a dog flea, *Ctenocephalides canis.*

S. E. M. BY DR DENNIS KUNKEL, UNIVERSITY OF HAWAII

Magnified head of a dog flea, *Ctenocephalides canis.*

S. E. M. BY DR DENNIS KUNKEL, UNIVERSITY OF HAWAII

A male dog flea, *Ctenocephalides canis.*

EXTERNAL PARASITES

Of all the problems to which dogs are prone, none is more well known and frustrating than fleas. Flea infestation is relatively simple to cure but difficult to prevent. Parasites that are harboured inside the body are a bit more difficult to eradicate but they are easier to control.

FLEAS

To control a flea infestation you have to understand the flea's life cycle. Fleas are often thought of as a summertime problem but centrally heated homes have changed the patterns and fleas can be found at any time of the year. The most effective method of flea control is a two-stage approach:

PHOTO BY JEAN CLAUDE REVY/PHOTOTAKE.

FLEA-KILLERS

Flea-killers are poisonous. You should not spray these toxic chemicals on areas of a dog's body that he licks, on his genitals or on his face. Flea killers taken internally are a better answer, but check with your vet in case internal therapy is not advised for your dog.

one stage to kill the adult fleas, and the other to control the development of pre-adult fleas. Unfortunately, no single active ingredient is effective against all stages of the life cycle.

LIFE CYCLE STAGES

During its life, a flea will pass through four life stages: egg, larva, pupa and adult. The adult stage is the most visible and irritating stage of the flea life cycle and this is why the majority of flea-control products concentrate on this stage. The fact is that adult fleas account for only 1% of the total flea population, and the other 99% exist in pre-adult stages, i.e. eggs, larvae and pupae. The pre-adult stages are barely visible to the naked eye.

THE LIFE CYCLE OF THE FLEA

Eggs are laid on the dog, usually in quantities of about 20 or 30, several times a day. The female adult flea must have a blood meal

before each egg-laying session. When first laid, the eggs will cling to the dog's fur, as the eggs are still moist. However, they will quickly dry out and fall from the dog, especially if the dog moves around or scratches. Many eggs will fall off in the dog's favourite area or an area in which he spends a lot of time, such as his bed.

Once the eggs fall from the dog onto the carpet or furniture, they will hatch into larvae. This takes from one to ten days. Larvae are not particularly mobile, and will usually travel only a few inches from where they hatch. However, they do have a tendency to move

ILLUSTRATION COURTESY OF BAYER VITAL GMBH & CO. KG

A Look at Fleas

Fleas have been around for millions of years and have adapted to changing host animals.

They are able to go through a complete life cycle in less than one month or they can extend their lives to almost two years by remaining as pupae or cocoons. They do not need blood or any other food for up to 20 months.

They have been measured as being able to jump 300,000 times and can jump 150 times their length in any direction including straight up. Those are just a few of the reasons why they are so successful in infesting a dog!

away from light and heavy traffic—under furniture and behind doors are common places to find high quantities of flea larvae.

The flea larvae feed on dead organic matter, including adult flea faeces, until they are ready to change into adult fleas. Fleas will usually remain as larvae for around seven days. After this period, the larvae will pupate into protective pupae. While inside the pupae, the larvae will undergo metamorphosis and change into adult fleas. This can take as little time as a few days, but the adult fleas can remain inside the pupae waiting to hatch for up to two years. The pupae are signalled to hatch by certain stimuli, such as physical pressure—the pupae's being stepped on, heat from an animal lying on the pupae or increased carbon dioxide levels and vibrations—indicating that a suitable host is available.

Once hatched, the adult flea must feed within a few days. Once the adult flea finds a host, it will not leave voluntarily. It only becomes dislodged by grooming or

EN GARDE: CATCHING FLEAS OFF GUARD

Consider the following ways to arm yourself against fleas:

• Add a small amount of pennyroyal or eucalyptus oil to your dog's bath. These natural remedies repel fleas.

• Supplement your dog's food with fresh garlic (minced or grated) and a hearty amount of brewer's yeast, both of which ward off fleas.

• Use a flea comb on your dog daily. Submerge fleas in a cup of bleach to kill them quickly.

• Confine the dog to only a few rooms to limit the spread of fleas in the home.

• Vacuum daily . . . and get all of the crevices! Dispose of the bag every few days until the problem is under control.

• Wash your dog's bedding daily. Cover cushions where your dog sleeps with towels, and wash the towels often.

MIXING CAN BE TOXIC

Never mix flea control products without first consulting your veterinary surgeon. Some products can become toxic when combined with others and can cause serious or fatal consequences.

the host animal's scratching. The adult flea will remain on the host for the duration of its life unless forcibly removed.

TREATING THE ENVIRONMENT AND THE DOG

Treating fleas should be a two-pronged attack. First, the environment needs to be treated; this includes carpets and furniture, especially the dog's bedding and

Opposite page: A scanning electron micrograph of a dog or cat flea, *Ctenocephalides*, magnified more than 100x. This image has been colourized for effect.

143

The Life Cycle of the Flea

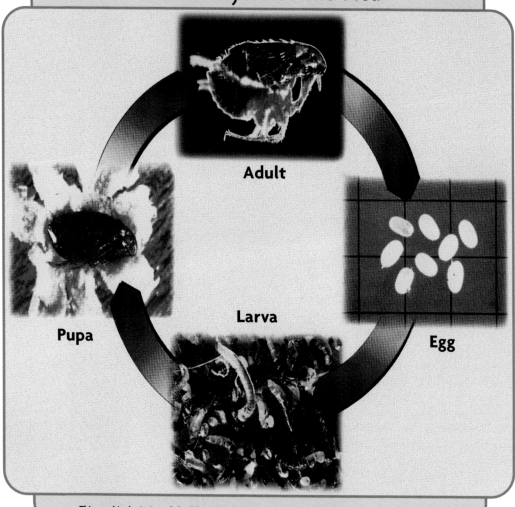

Adult

Pupa

Larva

Egg

This graphic depiction of the life cycle of the flea appears courtesy of Fleabusters®, R$_x$ for Fleas.

areas underneath furniture. The environment should be treated with a household spray containing an Insect Growth Regulator (IGR) and an insecticide to kill the adult fleas. Most IGRs are effective against eggs and larvae; they actually mimic the fleas' own hormones and stop the eggs and larvae from developing into adult fleas. There are currently no treatments available to attack the pupa stage of the life cycle, so the adult insecticide is used to kill the newly hatched adult fleas before

Photo by Dwight R Kuhn

TICKS AND MITES

Though not as common as fleas, ticks and mites are found all over the tropical and temperate world. They don't bite, like fleas; they harpoon. They dig their sharp proboscis (nose) into the dog's skin and drink the blood. Their only food and drink is dog's blood. Dogs can get Lyme disease, Rocky Mountain spotted fever (normally

Dwight R Kuhn's magnificent action photo showing a flea jumping from a dog's back.

they find a host. Most IGRs are active for many months, whilst adult insecticides are only active for a few days.

When treating with a household spray, it is a good idea to vacuum before applying the product. This stimulates as many pupae as possible to hatch into adult fleas. The vacuum cleaner should also be treated with a flea treatment to prevent the eggs and larvae that have been hoovered into the vacuum bag from hatching. The second stage of treatment is to apply an adult insecticide to the dog. Traditionally, this would be in the form of a collar or a spray, but more recent innovations include digestible insecticides that poison the fleas when they ingest the dog's blood. Alternatively, there are drops that, when placed on the back of the animal's neck, spread throughout the fur and skin to kill adult fleas.

FLEA CONTROL

Two types of products should be used when treating fleas—a product to treat the pet and a product to treat the home. Adult fleas represent less than 1% of the flea population. The pre-adult fleas (eggs, larvae and pupae) represent more than 99% of the flea population and are found in the environment; it is in the case of pre-adult fleas that products containing an Insect Growth Regulator (IGR) should be used in the home.

IGRs are a new class of compounds used to prevent the development of insects. They do not kill the insect outright, but instead use the insect's biology against it to stop it from completing its growth. Products that contain methoprene are the world's first and leading IGRs. Used to control fleas and other insects, this type of IGR will stop flea larvae from developing and protect the house for up to seven months.

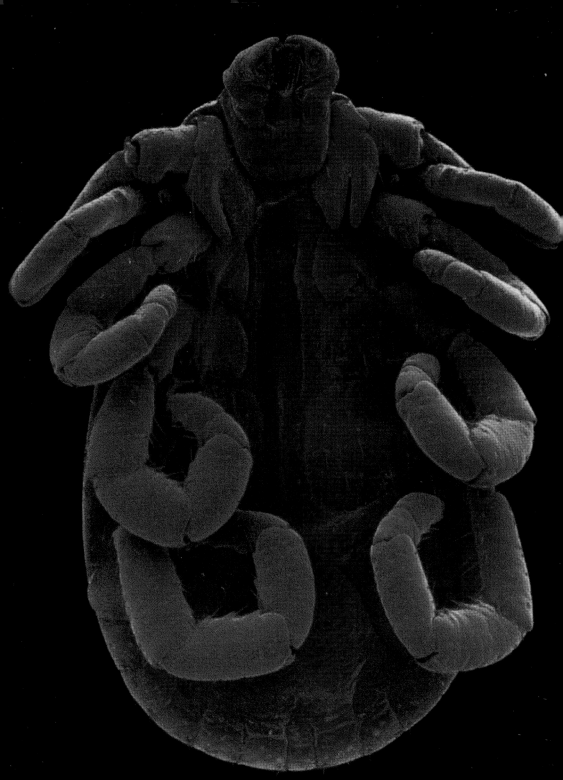

found in the US only), paralysis and many other diseases from ticks and mites. They may live where fleas are found and they like to hide in cracks or seams in walls wherever dogs live. They are controlled the same way fleas are controlled. The dog tick, *Dermacentor variabilis*, may well be the most common dog tick in many geographical areas, especially those areas where the climate is hot and humid.

Most dog ticks have life expectancies of a week to six

ILLUSTRATION COURTESY OF BAYER VITAL GMBH & CO. KG

Beware the Deer Tick

The great outdoors may be fun for your dog, but it also is a home to dangerous ticks. Deer ticks carry a bacterium known as *Borrelia burgdorferi* and are most active in the autumn and spring. When infections are caught early, penicillin and tetracycline are effective antibiotics, but if left untreated the bacteria may cause neurological, kidney and cardiac problems as well as long-term trouble with walking and painful joints.

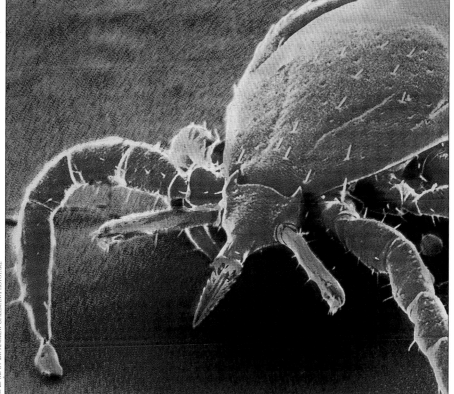

A deer tick, the carrier of Lyme disease. This magnified micrograph has been colourised for effect.

Opposite page: The dog tick, *Dermacentor variabilis*, is probably the most common tick found on dogs. Look at the strength in its eight legs! No wonder it's hard to detach them.

S. E. M. BY DR ANDREW SPIELMAN/PHOTOTAKE

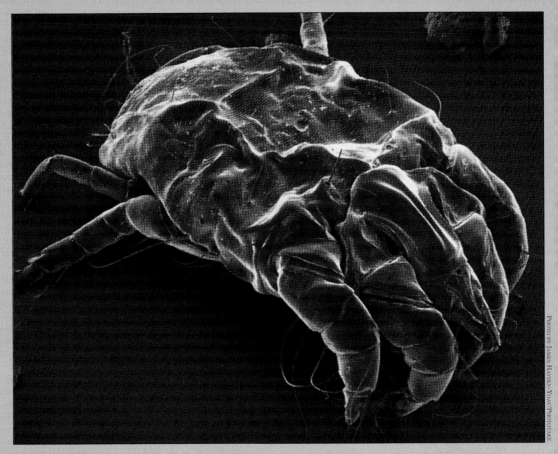

Photo by James Hayden-Yoav/Phototake

Above:
The mange mite,
Psoroptes bovis.

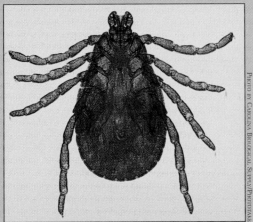

Photo by Carolina Biological Supply/Phototake

A brown dog tick, *Rhipicephalus sanguineus*, is an
uncommon but annoying tick found on dogs.

Photo by Dwight R Kuhn

Human lice look like dog lice;
the two are closely related.

months, depending upon climatic conditions. They can neither jump nor fly, but they can crawl slowly and can range up to 5 metres (16 feet) to reach a sleeping or unsuspecting dog.

MANGE

Mites cause a skin irritation called mange. Some are contagious, like *Cheyletiella*, ear mites, scabies and chiggers. Mites that cause ear-mite infestations are usually controlled with Lindane, which can only be administered by a vet, followed by Tresaderm at home.

It is essential that your dog be treated for mange as quickly as possible because some forms of mange are transmissible to people.

INTERNAL PARASITES

Most animals—fishes, birds and mammals, including dogs and humans—have worms and other parasites that live inside their bodies. According to Dr Herbert R Axelrod, the fish pathologist, there are two kinds of parasites: dumb and smart. The smart parasites live in peaceful cooperation with their hosts (symbiosis), while the dumb parasites kill their host. Most of the worm infections are relatively easy to control. If they are not controlled they weaken the host dog to the point that other medical problems occur, but they are not dumb parasites.

ROUNDWORMS

The roundworms that infect dogs are scientifically known as *Toxocara canis*. They live in the dog's intestine. The worms shed eggs continually. It has been estimated that a dog produces about 150 grammes of faeces every day. Each gramme of faeces averages 10,000–12,000 eggs of roundworms. There are no known areas in which dogs roam that do not contain roundworm eggs. The greatest danger of roundworms is that they infect people too! It is

DEWORMING

Ridding your puppy of worms is VERY IMPORTANT because certain worms that puppies carry, such as tapeworms and roundworms, can infect humans.

Breeders initiate a deworming programme at or about four weeks of age. The routine is repeated every two or three weeks until the puppy is three months old. The breeder from whom you obtained your puppy should provide you with the complete details of the deworming programme.

Your veterinary surgeon can prescribe and monitor the programme of deworming for you. The usual programme is treating the puppy every 15–20 days until the puppy is positively worm free.

It is advised that you only treat your puppy with drugs that are recommended professionally.

wise to have your dog tested regularly for roundworms.

Pigs also have roundworm infections that can be passed to humans and dogs. The typical roundworm parasite is called *Ascaris lumbricoides.*

HOOKWORMS

The worm *Ancylostoma caninum* is commonly called the dog hookworm. It is dangerous to humans and cats. It also has teeth by which it attaches itself to the intestines of the dog. It changes the site of its attachment about six times a day and the dog loses blood from each detachment, possibly causing iron-deficiency anaemia. Hookworms are easily purged from the dog with many medications. Milbemycin oxime,

ROUNDWORM

Average size dogs can pass 1,360,000 roundworm eggs every day.

For example, if there were only 1 million dogs in the world, the world would be saturated with 1,300 metric tonnes of dog faeces.

These faeces would contain 15,000,000,000 roundworm eggs.

It's known that 7–31% of home gardens and children's play boxes in the US contain roundworm eggs.

Flushing dog's faeces down the toilet is not a safe practice because the usual sewage treatments do not destroy roundworm eggs.

Infected puppies start shedding roundworm eggs at 3 weeks of age. They can be infected by their mother's milk.

The roundworm, *Rhabditis.* The roundworm can infect both dogs and humans.

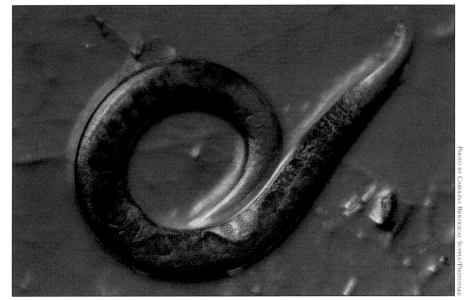

PHOTO BY CAROLINA BIOLOGICAL SUPPLY/PHOTOTAKE

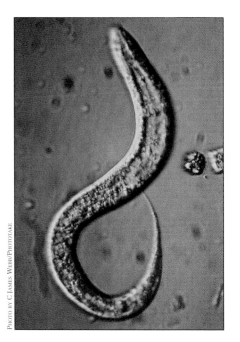

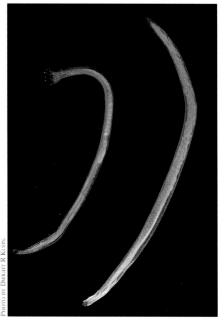

Left:
The infective stage of the hookworm larva.

Right:
Male and female hookworms, *Ancylostoma caninum*, are uncommonly found in pet or show dogs in Britain. Hookworms may infect other dogs that have exposure to grasslands.

which also serves as a heartworm preventative in Collies, can be used for this purpose.

In Britain the 'temperate climate' hookworm (*Uncinaria stenocephala*) is rarely found in pet or show dogs, but can occur in hunting packs, racing Greyhounds and sheepdogs because the worms can be prevalent wherever dogs are exercised regularly on grassland.

TAPEWORMS

There are many species of tapeworms. They are carried by fleas! The dog eats the flea and starts the tapeworm cycle. Humans can also be infected with tapeworms, so don't eat fleas! Fleas are so small that your dog could pass them onto your hands, your plate or your food and thus make it possible for you to ingest a flea which is carrying tapeworm eggs.

While tapeworm infection is not life threatening in dogs (smart parasite!), it can be the cause of a

CAUTION: NO SWIMMING!
Never allow your dog to swim in polluted water or public areas where water quality can be suspect. Even perfectly clear water can harbour parasites, many of which can cause serious to fatal illnesses in canines. Areas inhabited by waterfowl and other wildlife are especially dangerous.

The head and rostellum (the round prominence on the scolex) of a tapeworm, which infects dogs and humans.

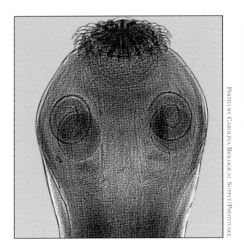

PHOTO BY CAROLINA BIOLOGICAL SUPPLY/PHOTOTAKE

TAPEWORM

Humans, rats, squirrels, foxes, coyotes, wolves, mixed breeds of dogs and purebred dogs are all susceptible to tapeworm infection. Except in humans, tapeworms are usually not a fatal infection.

Infected individuals can harbour a thousand parasitic worms.

Tapeworms have two sexes—male and female (many other worms have only one sex—male and female in the same worm).

If dogs eat infected rats or mice, they get the tapeworm disease.

One month after attaching to a dog's intestine, the worm starts shedding eggs. These eggs are infective immediately.

Infective eggs can live for a few months without a host animal.

Roundworms, whipworms and hookworms are just a few of the other commonly known worms that infect dogs.

very serious liver disease for humans. About 50 percent of the humans infected with *Echinococcus multilocularis*, a type of tapeworm that causes alveolar hydatis, perish.

HEARTWORMS

Heartworms are thin, extended worms up to 30 cms (12 ins) long which live in a dog's heart and the major blood vessels surrounding it. Dogs may have up to 200 worms. Symptoms may be loss of energy, loss of appetite, coughing, the development of a pot belly and anaemia.

Heartworms are transmitted by mosquitoes. The mosquito drinks the blood of an infected dog and takes in larvae with the blood. The larvae, called microfilaria, develop within the body of the mosquito and are passed on to the next dog bitten after the larvae mature. It takes two to three weeks for the larvae to develop to the infective stage within the body of the mosquito. Dogs should be treated at about six weeks of age, and maintained on a prophylactic dose given monthly.

Blood testing for heartworms is not necessarily indicative of how seriously your dog is infected. This is a dangerous disease. Although heartworm is a problem for dogs in America, Australia, Asia and Central Europe, dogs in the United Kingdom are not currently affected by heartworm.

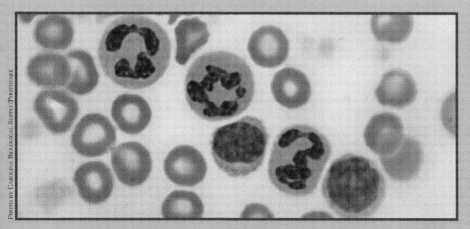

PHOTO BY CAROLINA BIOLOGICAL SUPPLY/PHOTOTAKE

Magnified heartworm larvae, *Dirofilaria immitis.*

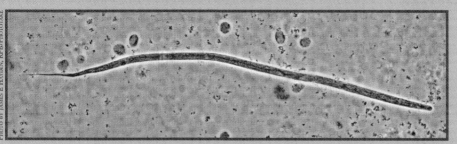

PHOTO BY JAMES E HAYDEN, RPB/PHOTOTAKE

The heartworm, *Dirofilaria immitis.*

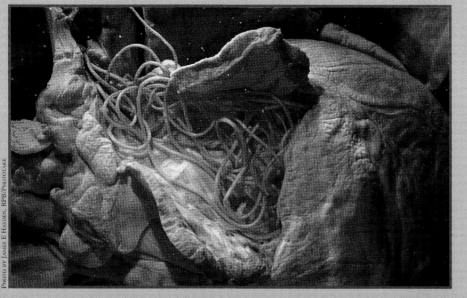

PHOTO BY JAMES E HAYDEN, RPB/PHOTOTAKE

The heart of a dog infected with canine heartworm, *Dirofilaria immitis.*

153

HOMEOPATHY:
an alternative to medicine

'Less is Most'

Using this principle, the strength of a homeopathic remedy is measured by the number of serial dilutions that were undertaken to create it. The greater the number of serial dilutions, the greater the strength of the homeopathic remedy. The potency of a remedy that has been made by making a dilution of 1 part in 100 parts (or 1/100) is 1c or 1cH. If this remedy is subjected to a series of further dilutions, each one being 1/100, a more dilute and stronger remedy is produced. If the remedy is diluted in this way six times, it is called 6c or 6cH. A dilution of 6c is 1 part in 1000,000,000,000. In general, higher potencies in more frequent doses are better for acute symptoms and lower potencies in more infrequent doses are more useful for chronic, long-standing problems.

CURING OUR DOGS NATURALLY

Holistic medicine means treating the whole animal as a unique, perfect living being. Generally, holistic treatments do not suppress the symptoms that the body naturally produces, as do most medications prescribed by conventional doctors and vets. Holistic methods seek to cure disease by regaining balance and harmony in the patient's environment. Some of these methods include use of nutritional therapy, herbs, flower essences, aromatherapy, acupuncture, massage, chiropractic, and, of course the most popular holistic approach, homeopathy. Homeopathy is a theory or system of treating illness with small doses of substances which, if administered in larger quantities, would produce the symptoms that the patient already has. This approach is often described as 'like cures like.' Although modern veterinary medicine is geared toward the 'quick fix,' homeopathy relies on the belief that, given the time, the body is able to heal itself and return to its natural, healthy state.

Choosing a remedy to cure a problem in our dogs is the difficult part of homeopathy. Consult with your veterinary surgeon for a professional diagnosis of your dog's symptoms. Often these symptoms require immediate conventional care. If your vet is willing, and somewhat knowledgeable, you may attempt a homeopathic remedy. Be aware that cortisone prevents homeopathic remedies from working. There are hundreds of possibilities and combinations to cure many problems in dogs, from basic physical problems such as excessive moulting, fleas or other parasites, unattractive doggy odour, bad breath, upset tummy, dry, oily or dull coat, diarrhoea, ear problems or eye discharge (including tears and dry or mucousy matter), to behavioural abnormalities, such as fear of loud noises, habitual licking, poor appetite, excessive barking, obesity and various phobias. From alumina to zincum metallicum, the remedies span the planet and the imagination…from flowers and weeds to chemicals, insect droppings, diesel smoke and volcanic ash.

Using 'Like to Treat Like'

Unlike conventional medicines that suppress symptoms, homeopathic remedies treat illnesses with small doses of substances that, if administered in larger quantities, would produce the symptoms that the patient already has. Whilst the same homeopathic remedy can be used to treat different symptoms in different dogs, here are some interesting remedies and their uses.

Apis Mellifica
(made from honey bee venom) can be used for allergies or to reduce swelling that occurs in acutely infected kidneys.

Diesel Smoke
can be used to help control travel sickness.

Calcarea Fluorica
(made from calcium fluoride which helps harden bone structure) can be useful in treating hard lumps in tissues.

Natrum Muriaticum
(made from common salt, sodium chloride) is useful in treating thin, thirsty dogs.

Nitricum Acidum
(made from nitric acid) is used for symptoms you would expect to see from contact with acids such as lesions, especially where the skin joins the linings of body orifices or openings such as the lips and nostrils.

Symphytum
(made from the herb Knitbone, Symphytum officianale) is used to encourage bones to heal.

Urtica Urens
(made from the common stinging nettle) is used in treating painful, irritating rashes.

INDEX

*Page numbers in **boldface** indicate illustrations.*

Acral lick granuloma 136
Activities 32
Adult diet 82
Age 103
Aggression
—fear 116
Agility trials 124
Allergy
—airborne 138
—auto-immune 136
—parasite bite 136
American Belgian Tervueren Club 24
American Journal of Cardiology 98
American Kennel Club 23, 45
Ancylostoma caninum 150, **151**
Ascaris lumbricoides **150**
Australia, 26
Axelrod, Dr Herbert R 149
Backpacking 123
Barking 34
Baronne 18
Basoef **11**, 16
Bedding 63
Behaviour 54
—puppy 54
Belgian Sheepdog Club of America 23
Belgian Sheepdog Club of Canada 24
Belgian Shepherd Dog Association 21-22
Belgian Shepherd Dog Club 9, 22
Berger Belge Club 11
Bergére 18
Blueprint of the Belgian Shepherd Dog, The 46
Boarding 96
Boer Sus **11**, 16
Bones 65
Bowls 67
Breeder 53, 58
—finding a 52
Britain 20
Brown dog tick **148**
Canada 24
Cat 111

Cataracts 42
Chaplin, Charlie **26**
Chateau Groenendael 18
Chewing 79, 107
Cheyletiella 149
Club du Chien de Berger Belge 9, 11
Club of Malines 13
Coat varieties 10
Collar 67, 112
—choke 67, 69
—choosing 69
Colostrum 81
Colour 56
Come 117
Commands 114, 119
Continental Shepherd 44
Cora van Optewel 14
Corbeel, M F 19
Coronavirus 135
Crate 62-64, 79, 94, 105-106
—training 63, 106
Crufts Dog Show 123
Crying 78
Ctenocephalides **142**, 143
Ctenocephalides canis **140**
De Bylandt, Count 44
De Groenendael **18**
De l'Ecaillon 12
Deer tick **147**
Dental health 133
Dermacentor variabilis **146**, 147
Development schedule 103
Dewet 11, 14
Deworming 149
—programme 149
Diane 14-15
Diet 80
—adult 82
—change in 86
—grain-based 81
—puppy 80
—senior 82
Dirofilaria immitis 153
Discipline 109
Distemper 135
Documents 55
Dog flea **140**
Dog tick **146**, 147
Down 114
Duc de Groenendael 18-19

Dutch Shepherd Dog 25
Ear cleaning 92
Ear mite 92
—infestation 92
Echinococcus multilocularis 152
Epilepsy 42
Excitability 34
Exercise 86-87
External parasites 140-149
Fairbanks, Douglas **26**
Fence 71
First aid 137
Flea **140-142**, 143, **145**
—control 145
—killers 141
—life cycle 141, **144**
—repellent 143
Food 80
—allergy 138
—intolerance 138
—preference 83
—proper diet 81
—storage 80
—treats 122
France 24-25
Gender 56
German Shepherd Dog 9, 21, 25, 44, **45**
Germany 25
Geudens, Dr G 10
Great Depression 23
Groenendael 11-12, 17
Grooming 87
—equipment 90
Health
—concerns 28
—dental 133
Heartworm 152, **153**
Heel 118
Hepatitis 135
Herding
—dogs 27
—tests 125
—trials 125
Hip dysplasia 39, 40
Hookworm 150-151
—larva 151
Housebreaking 101
—schedule 107
Housing 105
Huyghebaert, L 9, 18
Identification 97
Internal parasites 149-154
Ireland 22

Italy 24
Janssens 16
Japan, 26
Kennel Club, The 47, 55, 123
—standard 47
Kennel cough 131, 135
Kuhn, Dwight R 145
Laeken 16
Laekenois 11, 15
Lead 66, 112
Leptospirosis 135
Lice **148**
Lieske 15
Lindane 149
Lupus 136
Lyme disease 147
Malines 10, 13
Malinois 11, 13
Mange 149
—mite 148
Margot 18
Milk 81
Milsart 19
Mira 16
Mirza 18
Miss 19
Mite 145
Mouche 14
Nail clipping 92
Netherlands 24-25
Neutering 133
Night blindness 42
Nipping 78
Nutrition 85
Obedience class 98, 122
Obedience school 125
Parasite
—bite 136
—external 140-149
—internal 149-154
Parvovirus 135
Pastoral Group 27
Peggy de la Baraque de Planches 21
Personality 28, 30
Pet qualities 37
Petite 17, 19
Physical traits 28
Picard d'Uccle 17, 19
Pickford, Mary **26**
Pitt 18
Poes 19
Pollen allergy 138
Preventative medicine 129

PRA 42
Problems
—hereditary 38
—health 38
Progressive retinal atrophy 42
Psoroptes bovis **148**
Punishment 111
Puppy
—appearance 59
—behaviour 54
—coloration 56
—family introduction to 73
—financial responsibility 67
—first night home 74
—first trip to the vet 71
—food 80
—health 131
—home preparation 61
—needs 102
—ownership 59
—problems 75, 77
—selection 53-54
—show-quality 56
—socialisation 77
—training 99
Puppy-proofing 70
Quentin 21
Rabies 135
Registration
—early 11
Reul, Prof. Dr 9, 17
Rhabditis **150**
Rhipicephalus sanguineus **148**
Rose, Nicholas 17
Rottweiler 26
Roundworm 149, **150**
Royal Groenendael Club 11-12
Royal Society Saint-Hubert 11
Royal Union of the Belgian Shepherd Clubs 11
Samlo 14
Scandinavia 24
Schipperke **20**
Schutzhund 124
Senior diet 82
Sensitivity 33
Separation anxiety 78, 102
Sex 56
Sit 114
Skin problems 134
—auto-immune 136
—inherited 135
Socialisation 75-76
South Africa 26

South African Belgian Shepherd Dog clubs 26
Speciality show
—first 10, 17
Standard 43
—1892 10
—AKC 45
—FCI 45
—Kennel Club, The 45
Stay 115
Switzerland 24
Tapeworm 149, 151, **152**
Temperament 32
Tervueren 11, 14, 17-18
Thorndike's Theory of Learning 111
Thorndike, Dr Edward 110
Tick 145
Tjop 14
Tom 16, 19
Tomy 14-15
Tony 16
Toxocara canis 149
Toys 64-65
Tracheobronchitis 131
Training 36, 77
—begins 112
—consistency 110
—equipment 112
Travelling
—air 95
—auto 94
Treat 58, 112
Tresaderm 149
Type 44
Uncinaria stenocephala 151
United States 23
Vaccinations 73, 129
Van der Snickt, L 9
Varieties 11, 13, 28
—in the United States 23
Verbanck, Felix E 12
Versatility 28, 32
Veterinary surgeon 71, 127, 143, 149
Von Stephanitz, Max 9
Vos des Polders 11, 14
Vos I 15
Water 85
Whining 78
World War I 23
World War II 21, 24
Worms 56

My Belgian Shepherd Dog

PUT YOUR PUPPY'S FIRST PICTURE HERE

Dog's Name _____

Date _____ Photographer _____